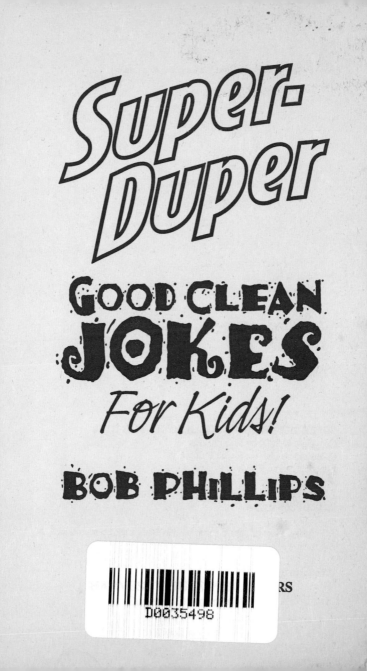

Super-Duper

Good Clean JOKES For Kids!

BOB PHILLIPS

D0035498

Cover by Terry Dugan Design, Minneapolis, Minnesota

SUPER-DUPER GOOD CLEAN JOKES FOR KIDS
Copyright © 2000 by Bob Phillips
Published by Harvest House Publishers
Eugene, Oregon 97402

Library of Congress Cataloging-in-Publication Data
ISBN 0-7369-0308-9

Printed in the United States of America.

00 01 02 03 04 05 06 / BC / 9 8 7 6 5 4 3 2 1

Contents

1

Jeff and Nole

Jeff: What do you get if you cross a centipede and a parrot?
Nole: I have no clue
Jeff: A walkie-talkie.

☆ ☆ ☆

Jeff: What's the smelliest city in America?
Nole: I don't know.
Jeff: Phew York.

☆ ☆ ☆

Jeff: What do you call a cattle tug-of-war?
Nole: I can't guess.
Jeff: Beef jerky.

☆ ☆ ☆

Jeff: What's the biggest ant in the world?
Nole: My Aunt Sophie.
Jeff: No, it's an elephant.
Nole: You obviously haven't met my Aunt
Sophie.

☆ ☆ ☆

Jeff: What is the brightest and most colorful
dog?
Nole: I have no idea.
Jeff: A paint Bernard.

☆ ☆ ☆

Jeff: What do you call a knight who just lost a
fencing match?
Nole: You tell me.
Jeff: A sword loser.

☆ ☆ ☆

Jeff: What should you do if you can't work
the lock on your door?
Nole: I give up.
Jeff: Sing until you get the right key.

☆ ☆ ☆

Jeff: What do you get when you cross a
     porcupine with a sheep?
Nole: Who knows?
Jeff: An animal that knits its own sweaters.

☆ ☆ ☆

Jeff: I bought a camouflage tent.
Nole: What's wrong with that?
Jeff I can't find it

☆ ☆ ☆

Jeff: What kind of dog goes "ticktock, tick
     tock, ticktock?"
Nole: You've got me.
Jeff: A clocker spaniel.

☆ ☆ ☆

Jeff: What kind of food did Romeo eat?
Nole: My mind is a blank.
Jeff: He ate what Juliet ate.

☆ ☆ ☆

Jeff: What is green, has four legs and can kill
     you if it falls onto you out of a tree?

Nole: I don't have the foggiest.
Jeff: A pool table.

☆ ☆ ☆

Jeff: What do you get if you cross a skunk
    with a hornet?
Nole: It's unknown to me.
Jeff: A smelling bee.

☆ ☆ ☆

Jeff: What do you call a camel without a
    hump?
Nole: I'm blank.
Jeff· Humphrey

☆ ☆ ☆

Jeff: What do you get if you cross a termite
    with a book?
Nole: Search me.
Jeff: An insect that eats its own words.

☆ ☆ ☆

Jeff: What's the best way to tell people they
    have bad breath?

Nole: I'm in the dark.
Jeff: By telephone.

☆ ☆ ☆

Jeff: What did the spider do inside the
    computer?
Nole: You've got me guessing.
Jeff: It made a web page.

☆ ☆ ☆

Jeff: What do you call a 100-year-old
    cheerleader?
Nole: How should I know?
Jeff: Old Yeller.

2

Funny Business

Who was Snow White's brother?
Egg White. Get the yolk?

☆ ☆ ☆

What were the Phoenicians famous for?
Blinds.

☆ ☆ ☆

Is it difficult to eat soup with a mustache?
Yes, it is quite a strain.

☆ ☆ ☆

Can any birds devour fish?
Yes, the pelican.

☆ ☆ ☆

Do you believe in heredity?
Sure, that's how I get all my money.

☆ ☆ ☆

If bees make honey, what do wasps make?
Waspberry jam.

☆ ☆ ☆

Have you heard the joke about the peach?
It's pitiful.

☆ ☆ ☆

Which is larger: a watermelon or a grapefruit?
They're the same! They both have ten letters.

☆ ☆ ☆

Which is the unluckiest monster in the world?
The Luckless Monster.

☆ ☆ ☆

Which animal has the highest intelligence?
A giraffe.

☆ ☆ ☆

I suppose you think I'm a perfect idiot.
Oh, none of us is perfect.

☆ ☆ ☆

Does your doctor make house calls?
Yes, but your house has to be very sick.

☆ ☆ ☆

Do undertakers enjoy their job?
Of corpse they do.

☆ ☆ ☆

Are there earthquakes on Mars?
No, but there are Marsquakes!

☆ ☆ ☆

Is there any word in the English language that
contains all the vowels?
Unquestionably!

☆ ☆ ☆

Is the skunk very talkative?
No, he's a creature of phew words.

☆ ☆ ☆

Why do elephants have flat feet?
They get them from jumping out of trees.

☆ ☆ ☆

Why do people laugh up their sleeves?
Because that's where their funny bones are.

☆ ☆ ☆

Why should the number 288 never be
    mentioned in company?
Because it is two gross.

3

I Want To Know Why

Judge: Why are you wanted in three states?
Criminal: I'm a popular guy.

☆ ☆ ☆

Teacher: Why didn't you write your report on
vegetables?
Student: I did, but my brother ate it.

☆ ☆ ☆

Mark: Why are bumblebees so hip?
Christy: I have no clue.
Mark: They know all the latest buzz words.

☆ ☆ ☆

Ryan: Why did you quit your job at the
    bubblegum factory?
Lisa: I bit off more than I could chew.

☆ ☆ ☆

Bob: Why is your clock laughing?
Pam: I guess it's ticklish.

☆ ☆ ☆

Tyler: How do you make a clock laugh?
Owen: I don't know.
Tyler: Tick-tick-tickle it.

☆ ☆ ☆

Detective: I'll find out who robbed the clock
    shop.
Robber: How?
Detective: Time will tell.

☆ ☆ ☆

Bud: Why was the physicist fired from his job?
Jan: I can't guess.
Bud: He had too many ions in the fire.

☆ ☆ ☆

Barry: Why did the trombone player go broke?

Stacey: I have no idea.

Barry: He let things slide.

☆ ☆ ☆

Jacob: Why did you cry when your brother got beat up?

Nathan: Because I'm my brother's weeper.

☆ ☆ ☆

Joshua: Why did Chiquita Banana go to see a psychiatrist?

Wally: You tell me.

Joshua: She had a banana-split personality.

☆ ☆ ☆

Jeff: Why did the king go to the dentist?

DeeDee: I give up.

Jeff: To get his teeth crowned.

☆ ☆ ☆

Emily: Why do elephants wear sneakers while jumping from tree to tree?

Lacey: Who knows?

Emily: They don't want to wake up the
neighbors.

☆ ☆ ☆

Ray: Why is it dangerous to go into the jungle
between two and four in the afternoon?

Sheila: I don't have the foggiest.

Ray: Because that's when elephants are
jumping out of trees.

☆ ☆ ☆

Matt: Why are pygmies so small?

Alisa: You've got me.

Matt: They went into the jungle between two
and four in the afternoon.

☆ ☆ ☆

John: Why did the writer enjoy working in the
basement?

Marci: It's unknown to me.

John: He was writing a best cellar.

4

Doctor, Doctor

Patient: Doctor, doctor, I keep dreaming there are great, gooey, bug-eyed monsters playing tiddledywinks under my bed. What shall I do?

Doctor: Hide the tiddledywinks.

☆ ☆ ☆

Patient: Doctor, doctor, I've got bad teeth, foul breath, and smelly feet.

Doctor: Sounds like you've got foot and mouth disease.

☆ ☆ ☆

Patient: Doctor, doctor, my husband smells like a fish.

Doctor: Poor sole!

☆ ☆ ☆

Patient: Doctor, how can I cure myself of
sleepwalking?
Doctor: Sprinkle thumbtacks on your bedroom
floor.

☆ ☆ ☆

Patient: Doctor, doctor, my wife thinks she's a
duck.
Doctor: You better bring her to see me
straightaway.
Patient: I can't do that. She's already flown
south for the winter.

☆ ☆ ☆

Patient: Doctor, doctor, I keep seeing green
and blue zebras.
Doctor: Have you seen a psychiatrist?
Patient: No, only green and blue zebras.

☆ ☆ ☆

Patient: Doctor, doctor, I keep thinking I'm a
trash can.
Doctor: Don't talk such garbage.

☆ ☆ ☆

Patient: Doctor, I think I'm a pin.
Doctor: I see your point.

☆ ☆ ☆

Patient: Doctor, I feel funny today. What
should I do?
Doctor: Become a comedian.

☆ ☆ ☆

Patient: Doctor, doctor, these pills you gave
me for BO . . .
Doctor: What's wrong with them?
Patient: They keep slipping out from under
my arms!

☆ ☆ ☆

A string bean took his friend, a pea, to the
hospital.
String Bean: How is he, doc? Can you save
his life?
Doctor: I have good news and bad news. The
good news is I can save his life. The bad
news is he'll be a vegetable the rest of his
life.

5

Knocked Out

Knock, knock.
Who's there?
Flea.
Flea who?
Flea's a jolly good feller.

Knock, knock.
Who's there?
Sherwood.
Sherwood who?
Sherwood like to come in, please.

Knock, knock.
Who's there?
Shirley.
Shirley who?
Shirley you have missed me.

☆ ☆ ☆

Knock, knock.
Who's there?
Dishes.
Dishes who?
Dishes the way I talk now that I've got false
    teeth.

☆ ☆ ☆

Knock, knock.
Who's there?
Doris.
Doris who?
Doris slammed on my finger and it hurts.
    Ouch!

☆ ☆ ☆

Knock, knock.
Who's there?
Emma.

Emma who?
Emma bit tired of knocking on this door.

☆ ☆ ☆

Knock, knock.
Who's there?
Justin.
Justin who?
Justin time. I'm getting cold out here.

☆ ☆ ☆

Knock, knock.
Who's there?
Oliver.
Oliver who?
Oliver sudden I feel sick.

☆ ☆ ☆

Knock, knock.
Who's there?
Stan.
Stan who?
Stan back—I'm going to kick the door down.

☆ ☆ ☆

Knock, knock.
Who's there?
Alec.
Alec who?
Alec my ice cream cone.

☆ ☆ ☆

Knock, knock.
Who's there?
Sid.
Sid who?
Sid down on the porch and rest awhile.

☆ ☆ ☆

Knock, knock.
Who's there?
Ken.
Ken who?
Ken you come out and play?

☆ ☆ ☆

Knock, knock.
Who's there?
Mr.
Mr. Who?
Missed her at the school bus.

☆ ☆ ☆

Knock, knock.
Who's there?
Luke.
Luke who?
Luke through the keyhole and you'll see.

☆ ☆ ☆

Knock, knock.
Who's there?
Ivor.
Ivor who?
Ivor a good mind not to tell you.

☆ ☆ ☆

Knock, knock.
Who's there?
Noah.
Noah who?
Noah good place to eat?

☆ ☆ ☆

Knock, knock.
Who's there?
I Etta.

I Etta who?
I Etta whole pizza for dinner.

☆ ☆ ☆

Knock, knock.
Who's there?
Omar.
Omar who?
Omar goodness, I forgot my key.

6

The Answer Man

Why has it taken you all morning to dig a
    foxhole?
I couldn't find a fox.

☆ ☆ ☆

Why did the teacher put corn in his shoes?
Because he had pigeon toes.

☆ ☆ ☆

Why did the fish go on a diet?
It weighed too much for its scales.

☆ ☆ ☆

Why was the computer so angry?
Because it had a chip on its shoulder.

☆ ☆ ☆

Why did the cannibal only eat thin people?
He was on a low-fat diet.

☆ ☆ ☆

Why did the butcher's assistant get fired?
He was caught choplifting.

☆ ☆ ☆

Why did the bees go on strike?
*Because they wanted more honey and shorter
    working flowers.*

☆ ☆ ☆

Why do bees have sticky hair?
Because of the honeycombs.

☆ ☆ ☆

Why did the lion sleep in a bowl of salad
    dressing?
So she would wake up really oily.

☆ ☆ ☆

Why was the broom late for work?
It overswept.

☆ ☆ ☆

Why did the music students get into trouble?
They were passing notes.

☆ ☆ ☆

Why was the frog down in the mouth?
He was unhoppy.

☆ ☆ ☆

Why did the trumpet player go to the dentist?
For a toot canal.

7

Barnaby and Basil

Barnaby: What do snowmen call their off-spring?
Basil: I have no clue.
Barnaby: Chilldren.

☆ ☆ ☆

Barnaby: What do you call a person who steals boats?
Basil: I don't know.
Barnaby: A shiplifter.

☆ ☆ ☆

Barnaby: What sort of fish performs surgical operations?

Basil: I can't guess.
Barnaby: A sturgeon.

☆ ☆ ☆

Barnaby: What material are you using to
build your puppy a home?
Basil: I have no idea.
Barnaby: Dogwood.

☆ ☆ ☆

Barnaby: What is the only breed of dog a
boxer is afraid of?
Basil: You tell me.
Barnaby: A Doberman puncher!

☆ ☆ ☆

Barnaby: What are students called who ride
the train?
Basil: I give up.
Barnaby: Passengers.

☆ ☆ ☆

Barnaby: What would you get if you crossed
an old rooster with a timepiece?
Basil: Who knows?

Barnaby: A grandfather cluck.

☆ ☆ ☆

Barnaby: What do most people do when they
see a rattlesnake?
Basil: You've got me.
Barnaby: They recoil.

☆ ☆ ☆

Barnaby: What do you get if you cross a
watch with a bedbug?
Basil: My mind is a blank.
Barnaby: A clockroach.

☆ ☆ ☆

Barnaby: What do Eskimos eat for breakfast?
Basil: That's a mystery to me.
Barnaby: Ice Krispies.

☆ ☆ ☆

Barnaby: What magazine do insomniacs read
in bed?
Basil: It's unknown to me.
Barnaby: *Snooze-week.*

☆ ☆ ☆

Barnaby: What do polar bears have for lunch?
Basil: I'm a blank.
Barnaby: Ice burgers.

☆ ☆ ☆

Barnaby: What's worse than a giraffe with a
sore throat?
Basil: Search me.
Barnaby: A hippopotamus with chapped lips.

☆ ☆ ☆

Barnaby: What would you get if you crossed
a baker with a prizefighter?
Basil: I'm in the dark.
Barnaby: A bread boxer.

☆ ☆ ☆

Barnaby: What did one ball of twine say to
the other ball of twine?
Basil: You've got me guessing.
Barnaby: Stop stringing me along!

☆ ☆ ☆

Barnaby: What do you call angry bacteria?
Basil: How should I know?
Barnaby: A cross culture.

☆ ☆ ☆

Barnaby: What do you call a python with a
great bedside manner?
Basil: Beats me.
Barnaby: A snake charmer.

8

Did You Hear?

Did you hear about the man who crossed a
carrier pigeon with a woodpecker?
*When the pigeon delivers the message, it can
knock on the door.*

☆ ☆ ☆

Did you hear about the man who crossed a
turkey with a centipede?
On Thanksgiving, everybody got a drumstick.

☆ ☆ ☆

Did you hear about the man who crossed an
octopus with a bale of straw?
He got a broom with eight handles.

☆ ☆ ☆

Did you hear about the Indian chief named
Running Water?
*He had two daughters—Hot and Cold—and a
son named Luke.*

☆ ☆ ☆

Did you hear about the Smogarian who won a
gold medal in the Olympics?
He took it home and had it bronzed.

☆ ☆ ☆

Did you hear about the Smogarian who found
some milk bottles in the grass?
He thought that he had found a cow's nest.

☆ ☆ ☆

Did you ever hear the rope joke?
Skip it.

☆ ☆ ☆

Did you know Larry's been fired from every
job he's ever had?
I guess nobody can call him a quitter.

☆ ☆ ☆

Did you ever see a sidewalk?
Me neither, but I've seen a nose run.

☆ ☆ ☆

Did you hear about the film star who had
many face-lifts?
*When she went for the next one they had to
lower her body instead.*

☆ ☆ ☆

Did you know you're walking the wrong
way?
This is the only way I know how to walk.

☆ ☆ ☆

Did you know he had false teeth?
Not until they came out in conversation.

☆ ☆ ☆

Did the teacher call on you in class today?
Well, she tried, but my cell phone was busy.

☆ ☆ ☆

Did you know I've never listened to an elastic band, but I've heard an engagement ring?

☆ ☆ ☆

Did you hear about the corn that got into a football fight?
He got creamed.

☆ ☆ ☆

Did you hear about the 100-year-old man who just died?
He died blowing out the candles on his birthday cake.

☆ ☆ ☆

Did you hear about the graffiti artist?
She retired because she saw the handwriting on the wall.

☆ ☆ ☆

Did you ever see a salad dressing?
No, but I've seen a bacon strip.

☆ ☆ ☆

Did you hear about the crazy water-polo
    player?
His horse drowned.

☆ ☆ ☆

Did you hear about the cross-eyed teacher?
He had no control over his pupils.

9

Rib Ticklers

Wife: You know the old saying, "What you
don't know won't hurt you"?
Husband: What about it?
Wife: You must really be safe.

☆ ☆ ☆

Sienna: Do you know the only fellow whose
troubles are all behind him?
Riley: I have no clue.
Sienna: A school-bus driver.

☆ ☆ ☆

Stan: Did you hear about the Indian named
Shortcake?

Linda: I don't know.
Stan: When he died, squaw bury Shortcake.

☆ ☆ ☆

Jared: You haven't touched your custard.
Andrew: Oh, you noticed.
Jared: Are you waiting for the fly to stop
     using it as a trampoline?

☆ ☆ ☆

Lindsey: Did you hear about the little boy
     who knocked on the door of the teachers'
     lounge and said, "Did anyone lose 50 dol-
     lars attached to a rubber band?"
Dorothy: No. Tell me what happened.
Lindsey: One of the teachers said, "Why, yes I
     did."
     "Well, today's your lucky day," said the
     boy. "I found the rubber band."

☆ ☆ ☆

Bruce: My dad is so old!
Sherry: How old?
Bruce: When he was at school, history was
     called "current events."

☆ ☆ ☆

Coach: Jackson, get in here.
Player: But, coach, I can't play today. I broke
    my leg.
Coach: That's a lame excuse.

☆ ☆ ☆

Bank: I'm afraid your checking account is
    overdrawn.
Man: That's impossible. I still have five
    checks left.

☆ ☆ ☆

Aunt: Will you let me kiss you if I give you a
    penny?
Nephew: A penny! Why, I get more than that
    for taking medicine.

☆ ☆ ☆

Romeo: Your cheeks are like petals.
Juliet: Really?
Romeo: Yes, bicycle pedals.

☆ ☆ ☆

Tim: What does your wallet look like after buying a computer?
Jenni: I don't have the foggiest.
Tim: Floppy.

☆ ☆ ☆

Rich: Last night my computer died.
Laurie: What did it die of?
Rich: A terminal illness.

☆ ☆ ☆

Man: Excuse me, but I'm registered at this hotel. Could you tell me what room I'm in?
Employee: Certainly, you're in the lobby.

☆ ☆ ☆

Candace: I hear you broke off your engagement. What happened?
Carly: Oh, it's just that my feelings for him changed.
Candace: Are you returning the ring?
Carly: Oh, no. My feelings for the ring haven't changed.

☆ ☆ ☆

Melba: I think I'll fix lunch.
Ken: I didn't know it was broken.

☆ ☆ ☆

Todd: Do you like the dictionary I bought you
    for your birthday?
Jill: Sure. It's a great present, but I just can't
    find the words to thank you enough.

☆ ☆ ☆

Bruce: I just read that forests cover 34 percent
    of the earth!
Juanita: Wood you believe it?

10

Where Me Out

Where did the elephant sign its contract for its
    TV commercials?
On the bottom.

☆ ☆ ☆

Where do snowmen put their money?
In the snowbank!

☆ ☆ ☆

Where do you take a sick wasp?
To the waspital.

☆ ☆ ☆

Where do you buy small chickens?
At the chick-out counter.

☆ ☆ ☆

Where do religious kids practice sports?
On the prayground.

☆ ☆ ☆

Where do people study volcanoes?
In the lavatory.

☆ ☆ ☆

Where would you find a prehistoric cow?
In a mooseum.

☆ ☆ ☆

Where do frogs keep their treasure?
In a croak of gold at the end of the rainbow.

☆ ☆ ☆

Where do biologists like to swim?
In the gene pool.

☆ ☆ ☆

Where can you find lots of shoes?
In the foothills.

☆ ☆ ☆

Where do fleas go in winter?
Search me!

☆ ☆ ☆

Where do computers go to dance?
The disko.

☆ ☆ ☆

Where do computers go to shop?
The hardware store.

☆ ☆ ☆

Where do the best bakers live?
On the Yeast Coast.

11

School Daze

Teacher: What explorer discovered that the
world was round?
Student: Sir Cumference?

☆ ☆ ☆

Teacher: Which president had the sharpest
teeth?
Student: I don't know!
Teacher: Jaws Washington!

☆ ☆ ☆

Teacher: Tell me something about the history
of the Iron Age.

Student: Sorry, but I'm a bit rusty on that one.

☆ ☆ ☆

Teacher: Who knows what a hippie is?
Student: It's something that holds your leggies on.

☆ ☆ ☆

Teacher: What would you do, Sam, if you found a million dollars?
Student: If it belonged to a poor person, I would give it back.

☆ ☆ ☆

Teacher: Stop your dreaming.
Student: I wasn't dreaming. I was taking a nap.

☆ ☆ ☆

Teacher: Why are you carrying a turtle to school?
Student: It would take him forever to walk.

☆ ☆ ☆

Teacher: I wish you would pay a little
    attention.
Student: I'm paying as little as possible.

☆ ☆ ☆

Teacher: Who was the first woman on earth?
Student: I don't know, sir.
Teacher: Come on, it has something to do
    with an apple.
Student: Granny Smith?

☆ ☆ ☆

Teacher: Not only is he the worst-behaved
    child in my class, but he also has a perfect
    attendance record!

12

Christy and Cornelia

Christy: What do you call a boy lying in the gutter?
Cornelia: I have no clue.
Christy: Dwayne.

☆ ☆ ☆

Christy: What kind of man doesn't like to sit in front of the fire?
Cornelia: I don't know.
Christy: Frosty the Snowman.

☆ ☆ ☆

Christy: What would you get if you crossed a newborn snake with a basketball?

Cornelia: I have no idea.
Christy: A bouncing baby boa.

☆ ☆ ☆

Christy: What kind of leash should you buy
for a mouse?
Cornelia: You tell me.
Christy: A short one!

☆ ☆ ☆

Christy: What do you get if you cross a glow-
worm with a python?
Cornelia: I give up.
Christy: A 20-foot-long strip light that can
squeeze you to death.

☆ ☆ ☆

Christy: What do you get when you cross a
Doberman with a bird?
Cornelia: Who knows?
Christy: A Doberman fincher!

☆ ☆ ☆

Christy: What kind of plates do skeletons eat
off of?

Cornelia: You've got me.
Christy: Bone china.

☆ ☆ ☆

Christy: What is the difference between a
baby-sitter and a psychiatrist?
Cornelia: My mind is blank.
Christy: One minds the babies and the other
babies the minds.

☆ ☆ ☆

Christy: What kind of clock does a kangaroo
carry?
Cornelia: That's a mystery.
Christy: A pocket watch.

☆ ☆ ☆

Christy: What's the hardest thing about falling
out of bed on the first day of school?
Cornelia: I don't have the foggiest.
Christy: The floor!

☆ ☆ ☆

Christy: What part of your body is the
noisiest?

Cornelia: It's unknown to me.
Christy: Your eardrum.

☆ ☆ ☆

Christy: What did the skeleton say to his girl-
friend?
Cornelia: I'm blank.
Christy: I love every bone in your body.

☆ ☆ ☆

Christy: What kind of fish do you eat with
peanut butter?
Cornelia: Search me.
Christy: Jellyfish.

☆ ☆ ☆

Christy: What sickness can you catch from
your mattress?
Cornelia: I'm in the dark.
Christy: Spring fever.

☆ ☆ ☆

Christy: What kind of hair do oceans have?
Cornelia: You've got me guessing.
Christy: Wavy.

☆ ☆ ☆

Christy: What do you call a bat in a belfry?
Cornelia: How should I know?
Christy: A dingbat.

☆ ☆ ☆

Christy: What do frogs drink?
Cornelia: Beats me.
Christy: Hot croako.

13

Belly Laughs

Boy: Little Joey finally ate his oatmeal.
Mother: How did you get him to eat it?
Boy: I told him it was mud.

☆ ☆ ☆

"Nobody likes me in school," he complained.
   "The teachers don't like me, the kids don't
   like me, the superintendent wants to
   transfer me, the bus drivers hate me, the
   school board wants me to drop out, and
   the custodians have it in for me. I don't
   want to go to school."
"But you have to go to school," countered his
   mother. "You are healthy, you have a lot

to learn, you have something to offer others, you are a leader. And besides, you are 45 years old and you are the principal."

☆ ☆ ☆

Mother: Judy, I have told you before not to speak when older people are talking. Wait until they stop.
Judy: I tried, but they never stop.

☆ ☆ ☆

Kid: Disgusting! There's a bug on my french fries!
Cafeteria Server: Don't worry, kid. The spider on your hamburger will eat it up in no time!

☆ ☆ ☆

Wife: I got up really early this morning and opened the door in my pajamas!
Husband: That's a funny place to keep a door.

☆ ☆ ☆

First Snake: I'm writing my hisstory.
Second Snake: I'm a writer, too. I write boa-
graphies.

☆ ☆ ☆

Mother: Were you a good boy in school
today?
Son: How much trouble can you get into
standing in a corner all day?

☆ ☆ ☆

It was a bright spring morning and four high
school boys decided to skip school. They
arrived at school after lunch and told the
teacher that their car had a flat tire along
the way, and that was why they were late.
To their relief, the teacher smiled and said,
"You boys missed a little test this
morning. Please take seats apart from one
another and get out your paper and
pencil."
When the boys were seated, the teacher said,
"Each of you please answer just one question: Which tire was flat?"

☆ ☆ ☆

Brother: I fell down yesterday.
Sister: Did you have a nice trip?
Brother: Yes.
Sister: Well, tell me about it next fall.

☆ ☆ ☆

Husband: Our family's descended from roy-
alty.
Wife: Who—King Kong?

☆ ☆ ☆

Jeweler: Hello, 911. I own a jewelry store
and an elephant walked in and sucked up
all my jewelry with his trunk and ran
away.
Police: Can you give me a description?
Jeweler: I can't really, because he had a nylon
stocking over his head.

☆ ☆ ☆

Man: I would like to purchase a pound of
nails.
Clerk: That will be two dollars plus tax.
Man: I don't want tacks, just nails.

☆ ☆ ☆

Beggar: Can you spare a dollar for a piece of
cake?
Woman: Cake? Most people ask for bread.
Beggar: Today's my birthday.

☆ ☆ ☆

There was once a man who always went to
work on an egg. One morning it wouldn't
start, so he phoned the AAA. They told
him to pull out the yolk. He did, and the
egg started. When he got to work, he
phoned the AAA to thank them for their
help, and told them his egg was all white
now.

☆ ☆ ☆

Principal: Give me three reasons you want to
become a teacher.
Student: June, July, and August.

☆ ☆ ☆

Son: Don't you like being a telegraph
lineman?
Dad: No, it's driving me up the pole.

14

Where, Oh Where?

Where do dogs practice singing?
The barking lot.

☆ ☆ ☆

Where do pigs go when they die?
To the sty in the sky.

☆ ☆ ☆

Where do large dinosaur pigs live?
In Jurassic Park.

☆ ☆ ☆

Where does a snail eat?
In a slow-food restaurant.

☆ ☆ ☆

Where did you buy your goose-feather comforter?
Downtown.

☆ ☆ ☆

Where do pigs live?
In a high-grime area.

☆ ☆ ☆

Where do frogs keep their coats?
In the croakroom.

☆ ☆ ☆

Where do whales look up definitions?
In a Moby Dicktionary.

☆ ☆ ☆

Where does an American cow come from?
Moo York.

☆ ☆ ☆

Where do ants eat?
In a restaurant.

☆ ☆ ☆

Where do cool mice live?
In mouse pads.

☆ ☆ ☆

Where do people who always have excuses
    end up?
In the Hall of Blame.

☆ ☆ ☆

Where do jellyfish get their jelly?
From ocean currents.

15

Lisa and Lola

Lisa: What do you call a boy who lies on the floor?

Lola: I have no clue.

Lisa: Matt.

☆ ☆ ☆

Lisa: Do you know what happened to the man in the plane crash?

Lola: No, I don't know.

Lisa: He got an airline fracture.

☆ ☆ ☆

Lisa: What is the strongest animal in the world?

Lola: I can't guess.
Lisa: A snail, because it carries its home on
its back.

☆ ☆ ☆

Lisa: What game did Dr. Jekyll like to play?
Lola: I have no idea.
Lisa: Hyde-and-seek.

☆ ☆ ☆

Lisa: What dog is always tired in London?
Lola: You tell me.
Lisa: An English sleepdog.

☆ ☆ ☆

Lisa: What do snakes write on the bottom of
their letters?
Lola: I give up.
Lisa: "With love and hisses."

☆ ☆ ☆

Lisa: What do they call a man who still has
his tonsils and appendix in his body?
Lola: Who knows?
Lisa: A doctor.

☆ ☆ ☆

Lisa: What did the cat say as it finished its
milk?
Lola: You've got me.
Lisa: This is the last lap.

☆ ☆ ☆

Lisa: What pirate flag does Captain Peanut
Butter fly above his ship?
Lola: My mind is blank.
Lisa: The Jelly Roger.

☆ ☆ ☆

Lisa: What is the study of back-to-school
clothes shopping called?
Lola: That's a mystery to me.
Lisa: Buyology!

☆ ☆ ☆

Lisa: What's the favorite magazine for
sailors?
Lola: I don't have the foggiest.
Lisa: *Ports Illustrated.*

☆ ☆ ☆

Lisa: What do you call an insect from outer space?
Lola: It's unknown to me.
Lisa: Bug Rogers.

☆ ☆ ☆

Lisa: What is the difference between the North and South poles?
Lola: I'm blank.
Lisa: All the difference in the world.

☆ ☆ ☆

Lisa: What army officer works in the coal fields?
Lola: Search me.
Lisa: The major miner.

☆ ☆ ☆

Lisa: What is a reptile's favorite movie?
Lola: I'm in the dark.
Lisa: *The Lizard of Oz.*

☆ ☆ ☆

Lisa: What's yellow, brown, and hairy?
Lola: You've got me guessing.
Lisa: Cheese on toast dropped on the carpet.

☆ ☆ ☆

Lisa: What do you get if you cross some ants
with some ticks?
Lola: How should I know?
Lisa: All sorts of antics.

16

Henrietta and Ruby

Henrietta: What do you call a dumb skeleton?
Ruby: I have no clue.
Henrietta: Bonehead.

☆ ☆ ☆

Henrietta: What do you get if you cross a
    snake with a pig?
Ruby: I don't know.
Henrietta: A boar constrictor.

☆ ☆ ☆

Henrietta: What's the difference between a
    zebra and a mailbox?
Ruby: I can't guess.

Henrietta: Well, I'm not sending you to mail
my letters.

☆ ☆ ☆

Henrietta: What did the arithmetic book say
to the geometry book?
Ruby: I have no idea.
Henrietta: Boy! Do we have our problems.

☆ ☆ ☆

Henrietta: What do you get if you cross a
skeleton with a famous detective?
Ruby: You tell me.
Henrietta: Sherlock Bones.

☆ ☆ ☆

Henrietta: What did the cocker spaniel say to
its bone?
Ruby: I give up.
Henrietta: It was nice gnawing you!

☆ ☆ ☆

Henrietta: What makes more noise than 22
screaming kids in a class?
Ruby: Who knows?
Henrietta: Twenty-three screaming kids!

✰ ✰ ✰

Henrietta: What did the necktie say to the
   hat?
Ruby: You've got me.
Henrietta: You go on ahead and I'll hang
   around.

✰ ✰ ✰

Henrietta: What kind of paper does a derma-
   tologist write on?
Ruby: My mind is blank.
Henrietta: A scratch pad.

✰ ✰ ✰

Henrietta: What would you do if a lion came
   after you at 60 miles an hour?
Ruby: That's a mystery to me.
Henrietta: I would do 70.

✰ ✰ ✰

Henrietta: What did Adam say when Eve fell
   off the roof?
Ruby: I don't have the foggiest.
Henrietta: Eavesdropping again!

☆ ☆ ☆

Henrietta: What would you get if you crossed
a frog with a little dog?
Ruby: It's unknown to me.
Henrietta: A croaker spaniel.

☆ ☆ ☆

Henrietta: What do you get with a computer
in Alaska?
Ruby: I'm blank.
Henrietta: A moose.

☆ ☆ ☆

Henrietta: What do you call a man with a car
on his head?
Ruby: Search me.
Henrietta: Jack.

☆ ☆ ☆

Henrietta: What did the leftovers say when
they were put into the freezer?
Ruby: I'm in the dark.
Henrietta: Foiled again.

☆ ☆ ☆

Henrietta: What do you call a story about a
cow that has a fairy godmother?
Ruby: You've got me guessing.
Henrietta: A dairy tale.

☆ ☆ ☆

Henrietta: What do you get if you cross a bee
with a doorbell?
Ruby: How should I know?
Henrietta: A humdinger.

☆ ☆ ☆

Henrietta: What did the principal do when he
found out the weight machine was stolen
from the nurse's office?
Ruby: Beats me.
Henrietta: He launched a full-scale investiga-
tion.

☆ ☆ ☆

Henrietta: What pirate told the most jokes?
Ruby: I have no clue.
Henrietta: Captain Kidd.

17

There's a Fly in My Soup

Customer: Waiter, waiter! There's a fly in my soup!

Waiter: Yes, sir, he's committed insecticide.

☆ ☆ ☆

Customer: Waiter, did you know this steak is half raw?

Waiter: So eat the half that's cooked.

☆ ☆ ☆

Customer: Waiter, there's a small slug on this lettuce.

Waiter: Sorry, sir, shall I get you a bigger one?

☆ ☆ ☆

Customer: This steak you brought me is rare.
　I said "well done"!
Waiter:　Thank you, sir. I don't get many
　compliments.

☆ ☆ ☆

Diner: What is that?
Waiter: That's a tomato surprise.
Diner: I don't see any tomato.
Waiter: That's the surprise.

☆ ☆ ☆

Waiter: We have fried liver, boiled tongue,
　stewed kidneys, and pigs' feet.
Diner: Don't tell me your ailments. I came in
　for a chicken dinner.

☆ ☆ ☆

Diner: Waiter, there's a fly in my ice cream.
Waiter: Let him freeze to death. It'll teach
　him a lesson!

☆ ☆ ☆

Customer: Waiter, I found a hair in my turtle
soup.

Waiter: How about that! The turtle and the
hare finally got together.

☆ ☆ ☆

Customer: Waiter, there's a button in my
salad.

Waiter: It must have come off while the salad
was dressing.

☆ ☆ ☆

Customer: Waiter, waiter! What's this dead
fly doing on my meat?

Waiter: I don't know, ma'am. It must have
died after tasting it.

☆ ☆ ☆

Customer: Waiter, waiter! There's a mosquito
in my soup.

Waiter: Don't worry, sir. Mosquitoes have
very small appetites.

☆ ☆ ☆

Customer: Waiter, waiter! My lunch is
talking to me!

Waiter: Well, you asked for a tongue sandwich, sir.

☆ ☆ ☆

Customer: Waiter, waiter, why is my apple pie
all mashed up?

Waiter: You did ask me to step on it, sir.

☆ ☆ ☆

Customer: Waiter, waiter! There's a dead fly
swimming in my soup.

Waiter: Nonsense, sir. Dead flies can't swim.

☆ ☆ ☆

Customer: Waiter, waiter! There's a wasp in
my dessert.

Waiter: So that's where they go to in the
winter.

☆ ☆ ☆

Customer: Waiter, waiter! There's a fly in the
butter.

Waiter: Yes, sir, it's a butterfly.

☆ ☆ ☆

Customer: Waiter, waiter! There's a slug in my salad.

Waiter: I'm sorry, sir. I didn't know you were a vegetarian.

18

Questions and Answers

Why did Humpty Dumpty have a great fall?
To make up for a terrible summer.

☆ ☆ ☆

Why did the vulture cross the road?
For a fowl reason.

☆ ☆ ☆

Why do you get a charge out of reading a
    newspaper?
Because it's full of current events.

☆ ☆ ☆

Why did the elephant come back to school?
He wanted to get an education so he could
get a better job. He was tired of working
for peanuts.

☆ ☆ ☆

Why did the cookie cry?
Because its mother had been a wafer too long.

☆ ☆ ☆

Why shouldn't you give a little girl spaghetti
at midnight?
Because it's pasta bedtime.

☆ ☆ ☆

Why can't the three bears get in their house?
Goldy locks the door.

☆ ☆ ☆

Why did the new teacher give Smart Alec an
A-plus?
Because he made a wisecrack!

☆ ☆ ☆

Why did the pea go to the psychiatrist?
It had a split personality.

☆ ☆ ☆

Why was the computer wearing shades?
To cover its windows.

☆ ☆ ☆

Why don't astronauts get hungry after being
blasted into space?
Because they've just had a big launch.

☆ ☆ ☆

Why did the Siamese twins get a traffic ticket?
For double parking.

☆ ☆ ☆

Why did Frosty the Snowman send his father
to Siberia?
Because he wanted frozen pop.

☆ ☆ ☆

Why was the lawyer angry?
He made a cross-examination.

☆ ☆ ☆

Who rides a dog and was a Confederate general during the American Civil War?
Robert E. Flea.

19

Odds and Ends

Professor: Give me three collective nouns.
Student: Flypaper, wastebasket, and vacuum
  cleaner.

☆ ☆ ☆

Jack: Eeew! Where are you going with that
  skunk?
Jill: To my gym class.
Jack: But what about the odor?
Jill: Oh, he'll get used to it.

☆ ☆ ☆

Boy: Is it true that an alligator won't attack
  you if you carry a flashlight?

Swamp Guide: That depends on how fast you carry the flashlight.

☆ ☆ ☆

Mother: Darling, you shouldn't always keep everything for yourself. I have told you before that you should let your brother play with your toys half the time.

Son: I've been doing it. I take the sled going downhill, and he takes it going up.

☆ ☆ ☆

Steve: I was brought up on Bach, Beethoven, and Brahms. What were you brought up on?

Suzy: Pablum.

☆ ☆ ☆

Conrad: Do you ever find life boring?

Rich: I didn't until I met you.

☆ ☆ ☆

Duke: See that bear rug on the floor? That bear was only six feet away when I shot him. It was either him or me.

O'Bannon: Well, the bear certainly makes a better rug.

☆ ☆ ☆

Neighbor: Haven't I seen you on TV?
Actor: Well, I do appear on and off, you
    know. How do you like me?
Neighbor: Off.

☆ ☆ ☆

Husband: Ouch! I bumped my crazy bone.
Wife: Oh well, comb your hair right and the
    bump won't show.

☆ ☆ ☆

Agent: What exactly do you do?
Actor: Bird impressions.
Agent: What kind of bird impressions?
Actor: I eat worms.

☆ ☆ ☆

John: Let's play a game of wits.
Cindy: No, let's play something you can play,
    too.

☆ ☆ ☆

Chris: It says in this book that Eskimos eat raw fish and blubber.

Kathy: I'm not surprised. You would blubber, too, if you had to eat raw fish.

☆ ☆ ☆

Employee: I've worked here for over 30 years, and I have never asked for a raise.

Boss: That's why you've worked here for 30 years.

☆ ☆ ☆

Russ: I would like to know how long couples should be engaged.

Kathy: Same as short couples.

☆ ☆ ☆

Glen: This lightning scares me.

Laura: Don't worry, it will be over in a flash.

☆ ☆ ☆

First Man: I would like to speak to the general.

Second Man: I'm sorry, but the general is sick today.

First Man: What made him sick?
Second Man: Oh, things in general.

☆ ☆ ☆

Girl: Mom, you know you're always worried
    about me failing math?
Mother: Yes.
Girl: Well, your worries are over.

☆ ☆ ☆

Mother: Eat your spinach; it's good for
    growing children.
Junior: Who wants to grow children?

☆ ☆ ☆

Jennifer: I have an aunt who lives near one of
    the Great Lakes.
Jon: Erie?
Jennifer: Not really, but she is a little strange!

20

Hector and Harlow

Hector: What do you get if you cross a nun and a chicken?
Harlow: I have no clue.
Hector: A pecking order.

☆ ☆ ☆

Hector: What do you call a skeleton that won't get up in the morning?
Harlow: I don't know.
Hector: Lazybones.

☆ ☆ ☆

Hector: What would happen if you dropped the Thanksgiving platter?

Harlow: Beats me.

Hector: It would be the downfall of Turkey, the overflow of Greece, and the destruction of China.

★ ★ ★

Hector: What is a skunk's favorite children's book?

Harlow: I have no idea.

Hector: Winnie the Phew.

★ ★ ★

Hector: What did the farmer say to the noisy vegetables?

Harlow: You tell me.

Hector: Peas, be quiet!

★ ★ ★

Hector: What is the best kind of dog to direct traffic at a busy intersection?

Harlow: I give up.

Hector: A pointer!

★ ★ ★

Hector: What do you call a bear who got caught in the rain?
Harlow: Who knows?
Hector: A drizzly bear!

☆ ☆ ☆

Hector: What do you call a big Irish spider?
Harlow: You've got me.
Hector: Paddy-long-legs.

☆ ☆ ☆

Hector: What do you call a man who's black and blue all over?
Harlow: My mind is blank.
Hector: Bruce.

☆ ☆ ☆

Hector: What was your favorite class so far?
Harlow: The third grade. I spent two years there.

☆ ☆ ☆

Hector: What sickness did Santa get going down the chimney?
Harlow: I don't have the foggiest.
Hector: The flue.

☆ ☆ ☆

Hector: What is a termite's favorite break-
    fast?
Harlow: It's unknown to me.
Hector: Oakmeal.

☆ ☆ ☆

Hector: What animal sleeps standing on its
    head?
Harlow: I'm blank.
Hector: Yoga Bear.

☆ ☆ ☆

Hector: What do you call a monkey that sells
    potato chips?
Harlow: I'm in the dark.
Hector: A chipmonk.

☆ ☆ ☆

Hector: What kind of car does Mickey
    Mouse's wife drive?
Harlow: Search me.
Hector: A Minnie-van.

☆ ☆ ☆

Hector: What would you get if you crossed a pig and a pickle?

Harlow: You've got me guessing.

Hector: A dirty dill.

☆ ☆ ☆

Hector: What's the first thing calves learn in school?

Harlow: I pass.

Hector: Reading, writing, and the alfalfabet.

☆ ☆ ☆

Hector: What is that strange feeling I have in my head?

Harlow: You probably have that empty feeling.

21

Crazy Thoughts

Do you file your fingernails?
Naw, I just throw them away after I cut them.

☆ ☆ ☆

In what month do people talk the least?
February.

☆ ☆ ☆

Do you know of any cures for insomnia?
Try talking to yourself.

☆ ☆ ☆

Do you believe in letting sleeping dogs lie?

No, they should tell the truth.

☆ ☆ ☆

Was the watch mad when it was insulted?
Yes, it was ticked off.

☆ ☆ ☆

Does the man in the moon eat a lot?
Not when he's full.

☆ ☆ ☆

Which two letters are rotten for your teeth?
D K.

☆ ☆ ☆

Which vegetable is a space villain?
Darth Tater.

☆ ☆ ☆

Do you have any spareribs?
No, I only have enough for myself.

☆ ☆ ☆

Do you exercise daily?
No, Daley can exercise himself.

☆ ☆ ☆

This loaf of bread is nice and warm!
It should be—the cat's been sitting on it all day!

☆ ☆ ☆

Did his speech have a happy ending?
Sure, everybody was glad it was over.

☆ ☆ ☆

In what country does a person never walk?
Iran.

☆ ☆ ☆

Do you use elbow grease when you shine
your shoes?
No, I use shoe polish.

☆ ☆ ☆

How can you jump off a 50-foot ladder and
not get hurt?
Jump off the first step.

☆ ☆ ☆

How do you warm up a room after it's been
painted?
Give it a second coat.

22

Open the Door

Knock, knock.
Who's there?
Lou's Inn.
Lou's Inn who?
Lou's Inn my patience and it's cold out here.

☆ ☆ ☆

Knock, knock.
Who's there?
Luke.
Luke who?
Luke out the window and you will see.

☆ ☆ ☆

Knock, knock.
Who's there?
Nana.
Nana who?
Nana your business.

☆ ☆ ☆

Knock, knock.
Who's there?
Arthur.
Arthur who?
Arthur any kids who can come out and play?

☆ ☆ ☆

Knock, knock.
Who's there?
Myth.
Myth who?
Myth you too.

☆ ☆ ☆

Knock, knock.
Who's there?
Wilma.
Wilma who?
Wilma be home in time to cook dinner?

☆ ☆ ☆

Knock, knock.
Who's there?
Howie.
Howie who?
I'm good. How are you?

☆ ☆ ☆

Knock, knock.
Who's there?
Chile.
Chile who?
It's chile out here on the porch.

☆ ☆ ☆

Knock, knock.
Who's there?
Gorilla.
Gorilla who?
Gorilla cheese sandwich, please.

☆ ☆ ☆

Knock, knock.
Who's there?
Dummy.

Dummy who?
Dummy a favor and stop these knock-knock
jokes.

☆ ☆ ☆

Knock, knock.
Who's there?
Betty.
Betty who?
Betty can't eat that whole plateful of tuna
noodle casserole!

☆ ☆ ☆

Knock, knock.
Who's there?
Iguana.
Iguana who?
Iguana hold my hand?

☆ ☆ ☆

Knock, knock.
Who's there?
Beezer.
Beezer who?
Beezer black and yellow.

☆ ☆ ☆

Knock, knock.
Who's there?
Anita!
Anita who?
Anita nother 50 cents so I can buy dessert!

☆ ☆ ☆

Knock, knock.
Who's there?
Pasture.
Pasture who?
Pasture bedtime, isn't it?

☆ ☆ ☆

Knock, knock.
Who's there?
Alli.
Alli who?
Alli want for Christmas is my two front teeth.

☆ ☆ ☆

Knock, knock.
Who's there?
Fanny.

Fanny who?
Fanny the way you keep saying, "Who's
there?" every time I knock.

☆ ☆ ☆

Knock, knock.
Who's there?
Teak.
Teak who?
Teak a peak out your windows and see who's
knocking.

23

Pam and Melba

Pam: What do you call a neurotic octopus?
Melba: I have no clue.
Pam: A crazy, mixed-up squid.

☆ ☆ ☆

Pam: What do you get if you cross a skunk
and an owl?
Melba: I don't know.
Pam: A bird that smells but doesn't give a
hoot!

☆ ☆ ☆

Pam: What happens when you sit on a tack?

Melba: Beats me.
Pam: You get the point.

☆ ☆ ☆

Pam: What would you do if you found a
bookworm chewing your favorite book?
Melba: Take the words right out of its mouth.

☆ ☆ ☆

Pam: What does a coach do for chickens
during halftime of their football game?
Melba: You tell me.
Pam: He gives them a peep talk.

☆ ☆ ☆

Pam: What kind of dogs are the best with
children?
Melba: I give up.
Pam: Baby setters!

☆ ☆ ☆

Pam: What did one whale say to the other
whale when he was in trouble?
Melba: Who knows?
Pam: I need kelp!

☆ ☆ ☆

Pam: What do you do if your nose goes on strike?
Melba: You've got me.
Pam: Picket.

☆ ☆ ☆

Pam: What do math teachers enjoy with their coffee?
Melba: My mind is blank.
Pam: A slice of pi.

☆ ☆ ☆

Pam: My school is so tough.
Melba: How tough is it?
Pam: My school is so tough, the school colors are black and blue.

☆ ☆ ☆

Pam: What do they call a pig that owns a million acres of property?
Melba: Wow! Talk about a ground hog!

☆ ☆ ☆

Pam: What did the mommy bee say to the
     naughty little bee?
Melba: It's unknown to me.
Pam: Beehive yourself!

☆ ☆ ☆

Pam: What do you call a computer that's
     mean and grouchy?
Melba: I'm blank.
Pam: A crab Apple.

☆ ☆ ☆

Pam: What animal has the smallest appetite?
Melba: I'm in the dark.
Pam: A moth. It just eats holes.

☆ ☆ ☆

Pam: What did the hen study in college?
Melba: Search me.
Pam: Eggonomics.

☆ ☆ ☆

Pam: What would you get if you crossed a
     weeping willow with a UFO?

Melba: You've got me guessing.
Pam: A crying saucer.

☆ ☆ ☆

Pam: What's yellow and highly dangerous?
Melba: I pass.
Pam: Shark-infested banana pudding.

☆ ☆ ☆

Pam: What do you get if you cross a skeleton
with a sheriff on horseback?
Melba: How should I know?
Pam: The Bone Ranger.

24

Tongue Twisters

Two tree toads tied together tried to trot to town twice.

☆ ☆ ☆

Bisquick, kiss quick.

☆ ☆ ☆

Six slippery, sliding snakes.

☆ ☆ ☆

Fat friars fanning flames.

☆ ☆ ☆

Jack Jackson Zachary.

☆ ☆ ☆

The judge judged Judd.

☆ ☆ ☆

Three terrible thieves.

☆ ☆ ☆

Tim, the thin twin tinsmith.

☆ ☆ ☆

Strange strategic statistics.

☆ ☆ ☆

Toy boat.

☆ ☆ ☆

Six slick saplings.

☆ ☆ ☆

Six gray geese on green grass grazing.

✫ ✫ ✫

Copper coffeepot.

✫ ✫ ✫

Ziggy Jazinski.

✫ ✫ ✫

Six shy soldiers sold seven salted salmons.

25

How About an Answer?

How many balls of string would it take to
   reach the moon?
Only one, if it were long enough.

☆ ☆ ☆

How do you honor a chestnut?
Give it a roast.

☆ ☆ ☆

How do you prevent break-ins at
   McDonald's?
With a burger alarm.

☆ ☆ ☆

How was that new restaurant you ate in?
It's terrible. It's so bad they can't give out doggy bags because it would be cruelty to animals.

☆ ☆ ☆

How can you tell a dogwood tree from an oak tree?
By its bark!

☆ ☆ ☆

How do you milk an ant?
First, you get a low stool . . .

☆ ☆ ☆

How do hot-dog contests come out?
Weiner take all.

☆ ☆ ☆

How badly were you hurt?
I don't know. I haven't seen my lawyer yet.

☆ ☆ ☆

How does an elephant get out of a small car?
The same way he got in.

☆ ☆ ☆

How come you broke up with your
    boyfriend?
*Because he ignored me. If there's one thing I
    can't stand, it's ignorance.*

☆ ☆ ☆

How do you make a Venetian blind?
Poke him in the eye.

☆ ☆ ☆

How did the fish get its nose fixed?
It went to a plastic sturgeon.

☆ ☆ ☆

How does a street organist like his job?
It's a grind.

☆ ☆ ☆

How did the basketball court get wet?
The players dribbled all over it.

☆ ☆ ☆

How did you get to the nurse's office?
Flu.

26

Tyler and Ryan

Tyler: What do you say if you meet a toad?
Ryan: I have no clue.
Tyler: Wart's new?

☆ ☆ ☆

Tyler: What's the best way to beat the flu?
Ryan: I don't know.
Tyler: With a stick.

☆ ☆ ☆

Tyler: What's a computer's favorite snack?
Ryan: Beats me.
Tyler: Chips.

☆ ☆ ☆

Tyler: What do you get if you cross an eagle
    with a skunk?
Ryan: I have no idea.
Tyler: A bird that stinks to high heaven.

☆ ☆ ☆

Tyler: What market do dogs avoid?
Ryan: You tell me.
Tyler: A flea market!

☆ ☆ ☆

Tyler: What's the difference between a com-
    puter and a piece of paper?
Ryan: I give up.
Tyler: You can't make a spitball out of a com-
    puter.

☆ ☆ ☆

Tyler: What does Luke Skywalker shave
    with?
Ryan: Who knows?
Tyler: A laser blade.

☆ ☆ ☆

Tyler: What happened when the wheel was
   invented?
Ryan: You've got me.
Tyler: It caused a revolution.

☆ ☆ ☆

Tyler: What do you get when you cross a
   computer with an icy road?
Ryan: My mind is blank.
Tyler: A hard drive.

☆ ☆ ☆

Tyler: What did the boy tornado say to the
   girl tornado?
Ryan: That's a mystery.
Tyler: Let's go out for a spin.

☆ ☆ ☆

Tyler: What is the first thing that bats learn at
   school?
Ryan: I don't have the foggiest.
Tyler: The alphabat.

☆ ☆ ☆

Tyler: What do you call an elephant who lies
   across the middle of a tennis court?

Ryan: It's unknown to me.
Tyler: Annette!

☆ ☆ ☆

Tyler: What do you call a musical instrument
that costs 1000 dollars?
Ryan: I'm blank.
Tyler: A grand piano.

☆ ☆ ☆

Tyler: What has four legs and flies?
Ryan: I'm in the dark.
Tyler: A picnic table.

☆ ☆ ☆

Tyler: What do you mean our financial situa-
tion is fluid?
Ryan: We're going down the drain.

☆ ☆ ☆

Tyler: What does a parrot do with a pencil?
Ryan: You've got me guessing.
Tyler: Polly doodles all the day.

☆ ☆ ☆

Tyler: What did one cannibal say to the other
as they ate the clown?

Ryan: I pass.

Tyler: Gee, he tastes funny.

27

Kevin and Cory

Kevin: What's that turtle doing in the school hallway?
Cory: I have no clue.
Kevin: About two miles an hour!

☆ ☆ ☆

Kevin: What do you call a pig with a bad sunburn?
Cory: I don't know.
Kevin: Baked ham.

☆ ☆ ☆

Kevin: What do you call an elephant who can't add and subtract?

Cory: Beats me.
Kevin: Dumbo.

☆ ☆ ☆

Kevin: What is hairy and coughs?
Cory: I have no idea.
Kevin: A coconut with a cold.

☆ ☆ ☆

Kevin: What is a pig's favorite song?
Cory: You tell me.
Kevin: "I Wanna Hold Your Ham!"

☆ ☆ ☆

Kevin: What did the tangerine say when it
     saw the Chihuahua?
Cory: I give up.
Kevin: Nothing. Tangerines can't talk!

☆ ☆ ☆

Kevin: What's at the center of earth?
Cory: Who knows?
Kevin: R.

☆ ☆ ☆

Kevin: What happened to the man who couldn't tell the difference between porridge and putty?

Cory: You've got me.

Kevin: All his windows fell out.

☆ ☆ ☆

Kevin: What happened to the boat that sank in the sea full of piranha?

Cory: My mind is blank.

Kevin: It came back with a skeleton crew.

☆ ☆ ☆

Kevin: What is a comedian's favorite cereal?

Cory: That's a mystery.

Kevin: Shredded Wit.

☆ ☆ ☆

Kevin: What do you get between sunrise and sunset?

Cory: I don't have the foggiest.

Kevin: Sunburned.

☆ ☆ ☆

Kevin: What do you get if you cross a
    policeman with a spider?
Cory: It's unknown to me.
Kevin: A copweb.

☆ ☆ ☆

Kevin: What kind of ant is good at adding up?
Cory: I'm blank.
Kevin: An accountant.

☆ ☆ ☆

Kevin: What do you get when you cross a
    movie with a swimming pool?
Cory: I'm in the dark.
Kevin: A dive-in theater.

☆ ☆ ☆

Kevin: What bird never goes to a barber?
Cory: Search me.
Kevin: A bald eagle.

☆ ☆ ☆

Kevin: What do you call a person whose car
    has been repossessed?

Cory: You've got me guessing.
Kevin: A pedestrian.

☆ ☆ ☆

Kevin: What do you call an alien starship that
    drips water?
Cory: I pass.
Kevin: A crying saucer.

☆ ☆ ☆

Kevin: What sort of a car has your dad got?
Cory: I can't remember the name. I think it
    starts with *T*.
Kevin: Really? Ours only starts with gas.

28

Tell Me Why

Why were you speeding?
I was late for traffic school.

⭐ ⭐ ⭐

Why don't you ever make me breakfast in
   bed?
Because I can't get the stove up the stairs.

⭐ ⭐ ⭐

Why did you move me up to the fourteenth
   floor?
You said you wanted a raise.

⭐ ⭐ ⭐

Why are you driving without a license?
Because it was revoked months ago.

☆ ☆ ☆

Why is the radio on?
'Cause I can't hear it when it's off.

☆ ☆ ☆

Why are the mouse's grades so low?
Because he doesn't squeak up in class.

☆ ☆ ☆

Why don't geese grow up?
Because they grow down.

☆ ☆ ☆

Why did they arrest the big cheese?
Its alibi was full of holes.

☆ ☆ ☆

Why did the tree see the dentist?
To get a root canal.

☆ ☆ ☆

Why did the kangaroo go to the doctor?
Because he wasn't feeling jumpy.

☆ ☆ ☆

Why does an elephant climb a tree?
To get in his nest.

☆ ☆ ☆

Why does the ocean roar?
*You would, too, if you had lobsters in your
bed.*

☆ ☆ ☆

Why should you always take a watch with
you when you cross the desert?
Because there is a spring in it.

29

Rupert and Roscoe

Rupert: What do you get if you cross a zebra
with an ape man?
Roscoe: I have no clue.
Rupert: Tarzan stripes forever.

☆ ☆ ☆

Rupert: What is the insect family's favorite
game?
Roscoe: I don't know.
Rupert: Cricket.

☆ ☆ ☆

Rupert: What did the tree say when it was cut
down?

Roscoe: Beats me.

Rupert: Well, I'm stumped.

☆ ☆ ☆

Rupert: What wild west hero makes noises
when he eats?

Roscoe: I have no idea.

Rupert: Wyatt Slurp.

☆ ☆ ☆

Rupert: What does a French poodle say
before each meal?

Roscoe: You tell me.

Rupert: Bone appetit!

☆ ☆ ☆

Rupert: What two letters can keep you from
doing your homework?

Roscoe: I give up.

Rupert: *TV!*

☆ ☆ ☆

Rupert: What kind of letters did the snake get
from his admirers?

Roscoe: Who knows?
Rupert: Fang mail.

☆ ☆ ☆

Rupert: What does the government use when
it takes a census of all the monkeys in
Africa?
Roscoe: You've got me.
Rupert: An ape recorder.

☆ ☆ ☆

Rupert: What do you call a guy who eats
meat, vegetables, and potatoes?
Roscoe: My mind is blank.
Rupert: Stu.

☆ ☆ ☆

Rupert: What kind of test do they give at
spider school?
Roscoe: That's a mystery.
Rupert: A Fly-Q test.

☆ ☆ ☆

Rupert: What kind of computer would you
find in the Garden of Eden?

Roscoe: I don't have the foggiest.
Rupert: Adam's Apple.

☆ ☆ ☆

Rupert: What do baby invisible zebras drink?
Roscoe: It's unknown to me.
Rupert: Evaporated milk.

☆ ☆ ☆

Rupert: What do you call a lion wearing
    headphones?
Roscoe: I'm blank.
Rupert: Anything you like. He can't hear you.

☆ ☆ ☆

Rupert: What is black and white and red all
    over?
Roscoe: I'm in the dark.
Rupert: A zebra with a sunburn.

☆ ☆ ☆

Rupert: What songs put baby birds to sleep?
Roscoe: Search me.
Rupert: Gullabies.

☆ ☆ ☆

Rupert: What do you call an insect that talks
a lot and then turns into a moth?
Roscoe: You've got me guessing.
Rupert: A chatterpillar.

☆ ☆ ☆

Rupert: What did one bat say to another?
Roscoe: I pass.
Rupert: Let's hang around together.

☆ ☆ ☆

Rupert: What is big and gray and puts quar-
ters under the pillows of baby elephants?
Roscoe: How should I know?
Rupert: The tusk fairy.

30

How About That!

Jeff: How did the crow cross the river?
Corrie: I have no clue.
Jeff: In a crowboat.

☆ ☆ ☆

Jim: How would you rank the food in the cafeteria?
Debbie: Why bother? The food's rank already.

☆ ☆ ☆

Annie: How come you broke up with your girlfriend?

Jesse: She started using four-letter words.
Annie: Like what?
Jesse: Like "Find some work."

☆ ☆ ☆

Paul: How did your Chihuahua break its leg?
Jorje: I dropped some dog food on it by accident.

☆ ☆ ☆

Elizabeth: How do you cure a headache?
Paulie: I can't guess.
Elizabeth: Put your head through a window, and the pane will disappear.

☆ ☆ ☆

Jessica: How did the farmer fix his jeans?
Jeremy: I have no idea.
Jessica: With a cabbage patch.

☆ ☆ ☆

Larry: How does the goat keep his hands warm?
Jackie: You tell me.
Larry: He has kid gloves.

☆ ☆ ☆

Cindy: How do you find out where a flea has bitten you?
Lloyd: I give up.
Cindy: Start from scratch.

☆ ☆ ☆

Jared: How were the hamburgers taken to the police station?
Alissa: Who knows?
Jared: In a patty wagon.

☆ ☆ ☆

Shane: How do you spell *wrong?*
Carrol: *R-o-n-g.*
Shane: That's wrong.
Carrol: That's what you asked for, isn't it?

☆ ☆ ☆

Amanda: How old would a person be who was born in 1917?
Taylor: Are we talking man or woman?

☆ ☆ ☆

Chris: How does an India rubber man travel?
Eric: You've got me.
Chris: In a stretch limo.

☆ ☆ ☆

Nancy: How did the carpenter break his
    tooth?
Bob: My mind is blank.
Nancy: Biting his nails.

☆ ☆ ☆

Jenny: How many times have I told you not to
    be late for dinner?
Ted: I don't know. I didn't think you were
    keeping score.

☆ ☆ ☆

Colson: How can you be such a perfect idiot?
Conner: I practice a lot by watching you.

☆ ☆ ☆

Chunk: How do snails get their shells all
    shiny?
May: That's a mystery.
Chunk: They use snail polish.

31

Silly Dillies

If a dog lost his tail, where would he get
another one?
At the retail store, naturally.

☆ ☆ ☆

If a man crosses the ocean twice without
taking a bath, what is he called?
A dirty double-crosser.

☆ ☆ ☆

If a man smashed a clock, could he be con-
victed of killing time?
Not if he could prove that the clock struck first.

☆ ☆ ☆

Who makes suits and eats spinach?
Popeye the Tailorman.

☆ ☆ ☆

Do deer enjoy themselves at parties?
Yes, they have a lot of fawn.

☆ ☆ ☆

Is the locksmith a good baseball player?
Sure, he's the key man.

☆ ☆ ☆

Which branch of the military does the most
    bragging?
The Boast Guard.

☆ ☆ ☆

Do you like soccer?
Yes, I get a kick out of it.

☆ ☆ ☆

I wonder where I got that puncture.
Maybe it was at that last fork in the road.

☆ ☆ ☆

Will you share your curds with me?
No whey.

☆ ☆ ☆

Did you make your bed?
No, I bought it.

☆ ☆ ☆

Are you in the top half of your class?
No, I'm one of the students who make the top half possible.

☆ ☆ ☆

Which is the meanest chicken in the yard?
Attila the hen.

☆ ☆ ☆

A rabbit's house is called a warren, alligators have nests, and foxes live in dens. What do you call your room?
A mess.

☆ ☆ ☆

Did you cut yourself?
No, it was a knife that did it.

☆ ☆ ☆

Did you just pick your nose?
No, I've had it all the time.

32

Stop That Knocking

Knock, knock.
Who's there?
Lionel.
Lionel who?
Lionel get you in trouble.

☆ ☆ ☆

Knock, knock.
Who's there?
Turnip.
Turnip who?
Turnip your hearing aid.

☆ ☆ ☆

Knock, knock.
Who's there?
Heaven.
Heaven who?
Heaven seen you for ages.

☆ ☆ ☆

Knock, knock.
Who's there?
Stu.
Stu who?
Stu late I'm leaving.

☆ ☆ ☆

Knock, knock.
Who's there?
Eva.
Eva who?
Eva you don't open the door you won't find
    out.

☆ ☆ ☆

Knock, knock.
Who's there?
Major.
Major who?
Major answer, didn't I?

☆ ☆ ☆

Knock, knock.
Who's there?
Jester.
Jester who?
Jester minute. I'm trying to find my key.

Knock, knock.
Who's there?
Dishes.
Dishes who?
Dishes a very bad knock-knock joke.

☆ ☆ ☆

Knock, knock.
Who's there?
Tennis.
Tennis who?
Tennis two plus eight.

☆ ☆ ☆

Knock, knock.
Who's there?
Police.

Police who?
Police open up the door.

☆ ☆ ☆

Knock, knock.
Who's there?
You.
You who?
Did you call?

☆ ☆ ☆

Knock, knock.
Who's there?
Isaac.
Isaac who?
Isaac coming in!

☆ ☆ ☆

Knock, knock.
Who's there?
Ya.
Ya who?
I didn't know you were a cowboy!

☆ ☆ ☆

Knock, knock.
Who's there?
Emma.
Emma who?
Emma bit tired and need to lie down.

☆ ☆ ☆

Knock, knock.
Who's there?
Ken.
Ken who?
Ken you find someone to open the door?

☆ ☆ ☆

Knock, knock.
Who's there?
Owl.
Owl who?
Owl be sad if you don't let me in.

☆ ☆ ☆

Knock, knock.
Who's there?
Pig.
Pig who?
Pig on someone your own size!

☆ ☆ ☆

Knock, knock.
Who's there?
Annette.
Annette who?
Annette is what I use to catch butterflies.

33

Jon-Mark and Jonas

Jon-Mark: What do bees do if they want to use public transport?
Jonas: I have no clue.
Jon-Mark: Wait at a buzz stop.

☆ ☆ ☆

Jon-Mark: What do you call a man in Nome who gets sunburned?
Jonas: I don't know.
Jon-Mark: A baked Alaskan.

☆ ☆ ☆

Jon-Mark: What do you call an 80-year-old ant?

Jonas: Beats me.
Jon-Mark: An antique.

☆ ☆ ☆

Jon-Mark: What do you get if you cross a
computer with an elephant?
Jonas: I have no idea.
Jon-Mark: Lots of memory.

☆ ☆ ☆

Jon-Mark: What is the favorite sport of a
mouse?
Jonas: You tell me.
Jon-Mark: Miniature golf!

☆ ☆ ☆

Jon-Mark: What is the best city to go bike-
riding in?
Jonas: I give up.
Jon-Mark: Wheeling, West Virginia.

☆ ☆ ☆

Jon-Mark: What's wrong with your pencil?
Jonas: It got a leadache!

☆ ☆ ☆

Jon-Mark: What do you get if you cross a
    skeleton with a famous detective?
Jonas: You've got me.
Jon-Mark: Sherlock Bones.

☆ ☆ ☆

Jon-Mark: What happens if you don't use the
    Internet for a while?
Jonas: My mind is blank.
Jon-Mark: Your computer gets cobwebs.

☆ ☆ ☆

Jon-Mark: What do policemen eat in Chinese
    restaurants?
Jonas: That's a mystery.
Jon-Mark: Copsuey.

☆ ☆ ☆

Jon-Mark: What is the singing dog's favorite
    movie?
Jonas: I don't have the foggiest.
Jon-Mark: *The Hound of Music.*

☆ ☆ ☆

Jon-Mark: What do you call two web sites that get married?

Jonas: It's unknown to me.

Jon-Mark: The newlywebs.

☆ ☆ ☆

Jon-Mark: What do you get if you cross a toad with a mist?

Jonas: I'm blank.

Jon-Mark: Kermit the Fog.

☆ ☆ ☆

Jon-Mark: What happens if you sit on a grape?

Jonas: I'm in the dark.

Jon-Mark: It gives out a little wine.

☆ ☆ ☆

Jon-Mark: What would you get if you crossed a doctor with a hyena?

Jonas: Search me.

Jon-Mark: A physician who laughs all the way to the bank.

☆ ☆ ☆

Jon-Mark: What did one blackbird say to the
  other blackbird?
Jonas: You've got me guessing.
Jon-Mark: Crow up!

Jon-Mark: What do you do when two snails
  have a fight?
Jonas: I pass.
Jon-Mark: Leave them to slug it out.

34

Tell Me How

How is it that every time I come around
you're not working?
You wear sneakers.

☆ ☆ ☆

How do trees fight?
They have a tree-for-all.

☆ ☆ ☆

How do you put an elephant in a mailbox?
Put him in a stamped envelope.

☆ ☆ ☆

How does the leopard keep house?
Spotless.

☆ ☆ ☆

How much do used batteries cost?
Nothing—they are free of charge.

☆ ☆ ☆

How does the man in the moon hold up his pants?
With an asteroid belt!

☆ ☆ ☆

How come the man died when he was shot in the finger?
He was scratching his head at the time.

☆ ☆ ☆

How did the dinosaur file its nails?
Alphabetically.

☆ ☆ ☆

How do you tell the difference between a mouse and a hippopotamus?

Try picking them up.

☆ ☆ ☆

How can you be sure to start a fire with two
   sticks?
Make sure one of them is a match.

☆ ☆ ☆

How do you catch a runaway computer?
With an Internet!

☆ ☆ ☆

How do you tune these "hard rock" instru-
   ments?
You don't.

☆ ☆ ☆

How do kittens shop?
From catalogs.

☆ ☆ ☆

How does an angel answer the phone?
"Halo."

☆ ☆ ☆

How do you stop a mouse from squeaking?
Oil it.

☆ ☆ ☆

How about a date on Saturday night?
*I can't see you on Saturday night. I'm
expecting a headache.*

☆ ☆ ☆

How many days of the week start with the
letter *T*?
*Four: Tuesday, Thursday, today, and
tomorrow.*

35

Grab Bag

A small boy was trying to explain a broken
window to a policeman: "I was cleaning
my slingshot, and it went off."

★ ★ ★

Kent: Don't be afraid of my dog. You know
the old proverb, "A barking dog never
bites."
Sylvia: Yes, you know the proverb, and I
know the proverb, but does your dog know
the proverb?

★ ★ ★

Student: I hear that fish is brain food.
Roommate: Yeah, I eat it all the time.
Student: Well, there goes another theory.

☆ ☆ ☆

Daughter: Dad, where is the Taj Mahal?
Father: Ask your mother. She puts everything
    away.

☆ ☆ ☆

Good news! I've been given a goldfish for my
    birthday. The bad news is that I don't get
    the bowl until my next birthday!

☆ ☆ ☆

Curtis: Have you heard the joke about the
    slippery eel?
Tim: No. What about it?
Curtis: You wouldn't grasp it.

☆ ☆ ☆

Connie: I can't decide if I should become a
    barber or write short stories.
Bob: Flip a coin: heads or tales.

☆ ☆ ☆

Sonny: Your face looks familiar.
Samantha: Of course. I've always looked this
way.

☆ ☆ ☆

Bad news: The crops have failed and we have
nothing to eat but lizards.
Good news: There aren't enough to go around.

☆ ☆ ☆

A police officer saw a man dressed as a
cowboy in the street, complete with huge
Stetson hat, spurs, and six-shooters.
"Excuse me, sir," said the police officer, "who
are you?"
"My name's Tex, officer," said the cowboy.
"Tex, eh?" said the police officer, "Are you
from Texas?"
"Nope, Louisiana."
"Louisiana?
"So why are you called Tex?"
"Don't want to be called Louise, do I?"

☆ ☆ ☆

Richard: I'm a coin collector. Are you?

Rich: Yes. Let's get together and talk over
old dimes.

Chuck: I play the violin and tell jokes at the
same time.

Martha: How can you tell what the people are
laughing at?

That joke was so old when I first heard it, the
Dead Sea was only sick.

The food in our school cafeteria is so bad that
even the flies have to see the nurse.

Dick: Joe swallowed a dictionary.

Joy: How's he doing?

Dick: I don't know. We can't get a word out
of him.

☆ ☆ ☆

Farmer Brown: What happened when the
   wooden sundial was left out in the rain?
Farmer Green: You tell me.
Farmer Brown: There was a time warp.

☆ ☆ ☆

Advertisement: Dog for sale. Really gentle.
   Eats anything. Especially fond of children.

☆ ☆ ☆

Mother: We don't have any more pancakes
   for breakfast!
Daughter: How waffle!

☆ ☆ ☆

Avi: Reading always makes me hungry!
Patrick: What kinds of things are you
   reading?
Avi: Menus.

36

Use the Doorbell

Knock, knock.
Who's there?
Atch.
Atch who?
God bless you. I didn't know you had a cold.

☆ ☆ ☆

Knock, knock.
Who's there?
Noah.
Noah who?
Noah don't know who you are either.

✩ ✩ ✩

Knock, knock.
Who's there?
Tennis.
Tennis who?
Tennis what comes after eight and nine.

✩ ✩ ✩

Knock, knock.
Who's there?
Bat.
Bat who?
Bat you'll never guess!

✩ ✩ ✩

Knock, knock.
Who's there?
Theodore.
Theodore who?
Theodore is shut. Please open it!

✩ ✩ ✩

Knock, knock.
Who's there?
Francis.

Francis who?
Francis where they have the Eiffel Tower.

☆ ☆ ☆

Knock, knock.
Who's there?
Icon.
Icon who?
Icon make you open the door.

☆ ☆ ☆

Knock, knock.
Who's there?
Oscar.
Oscar who?
Oscar silly question, get a silly answer.

☆ ☆ ☆

Knock, knock.
Who's there?
Lionel.
Lionel who?
Lionel about not knowing me won't help.

Knock, knock.
Who's there?
Cows.
Cows who?
Cows go moo, not who.

☆ ☆ ☆

Knock, knock.
Who's there?
Doris.
Doris who?
Doris locked and I can't get in.

☆ ☆ ☆

Knock, knock.
Who's there?
Yvonne.
Yvonne who?
Yvonne to be alone!

☆ ☆ ☆

Knock, knock.
Who's there?
Viper.
Viper who?
Viper your nose—it's running.

37

Winifred and Myrtle

Winifred: What do you call a multistory pigpen?
Myrtle: I have no clue.
Winifred: A styscraper.

☆ ☆ ☆

Winifred: What do you call a highly skilled
plumber?
Myrtle: I don't know.
Winifred: A drain surgeon.

☆ ☆ ☆

Winifred: What do you call an ostrich at the
North Pole?

Myrtle: Beats me.
Winifred: Lost.

☆ ☆ ☆

Winifred: What's red and green and wears
boxing gloves?
Myrtle: I have no idea.
Winifred: A fruit punch.

☆ ☆ ☆

Winifred: What's red and flies and wobbles at
the same time?
Myrtle: You tell me.
Winifred: A Jell-O-copter.

☆ ☆ ☆

Winifred: What is a dog's favorite breakfast?
Myrtle: I give up.
Winifred: Pooched eggs!

☆ ☆ ☆

Winifred: What did the frog order for lunch?
Myrtle: Who knows?
Winifred: A hamburger with flies.

☆ ☆ ☆

Winifred: What's the difference between a
  nail and a boxer?
Myrtle: You've got me.
Winifred: One gets knocked in, and the other
  gets knocked out.

☆ ☆ ☆

Winifred: What book contains more stirring
  pages than any other book?
Myrtle: My mind is blank.
Winifred: A cookbook.

☆ ☆ ☆

Winifred: What is the difference between an
  exhausted runner and a burned-out veterinarian?
Myrtle: That's a mystery.
Winifred: One is dog-tired, and the other is
  tired of dogs.

☆ ☆ ☆

Winifred: What did the hog say when he
  heard a pig joke?

Myrtle: I don't have the foggiest.
Winifred: Now that's squeally funny.

☆ ☆ ☆

Winifred: What does a pig do for bad breath?
Myrtle: It's unknown to me.
Winifred: It gargles with hogwash.

☆ ☆ ☆

Winifred: What did the mommy snake say to
the crying baby snake?
Myrtle: I'm in the dark.
Winifred: Stop crying and viper your nose.

☆ ☆ ☆

Winifred: What do computer couples fight
about?
Myrtle: Search me.
Winifred: Who has to take out the trash.

☆ ☆ ☆

Winifred: What is another name for a
nursery?
Myrtle: You've got me guessing.
Winifred: Bawlroom.

☆ ☆ ☆

Winifred: What starts out red and ends up black?
Myrtle: I pass.
Winifred: Santa Claus going down a chimney.

☆ ☆ ☆

Winifred: What kind of shoes do frogs like?
Myrtle: How should I know?
Winifred: Open-toad sandals.

☆ ☆ ☆

Winifred: What did the computer trio sing
    when the lights went out?
Myrtle: Beats me.
Winifred: "Three Blind Mice."

☆ ☆ ☆

Winifred: What does a rabbit do in the hot
    weather?
Myrtle: I have no clue.
Winifred: It puts on the hare conditioner.

38

When, When, When?

When rain falls, does it ever get up again?
Yes, in dew time.

☆ ☆ ☆

When you jumped down the stairs, did the
  ground break your fall?
No, it broke my leg.

☆ ☆ ☆

When do people who yell a lot celebrate?
On hollerdays.

☆ ☆ ☆

When is hot soup not hot soup?
When it's chili.

☆ ☆ ☆

When does the moon beam?
When you give it a compliment.

☆ ☆ ☆

When is it unlucky to see a black cat?
When you're a mouse.

☆ ☆ ☆

When will my ship come in?
Schooner or later.

☆ ☆ ☆

When is the best time to have lunch?
After breakfast.

☆ ☆ ☆

When is the best time to buy a pirate ship?
When there's a sail on it.

☆ ☆ ☆

When do skunks smell?
When they don't take a bath!

☆ ☆ ☆

When Lee ate raw onions for a week, what
did he become?
Lone Lee.

☆ ☆ ☆

When did you lose your notebook?
When I couldn't find it anymore.

☆ ☆ ☆

I have two noses, three eyes, and only one ear.
What am I?
Very ugly.

39

Chuckles

Trixie: When I die I'm going to leave my brain to science.
Tracey: I suppose every little bit helps.

☆ ☆ ☆

Grandfather: When I was a young man I thought nothing of a ten-mile walk.
Grandson: Well, I don't think much of it, either.

☆ ☆ ☆

Motorist: When I bought this car you told me it was rust-free, but underneath it's covered with rust.

Dealer: Yes, sir. The car is rust-free. We
didn't charge you for the rust, did we?

☆ ☆ ☆

Sister: When you leave school, you should
become a bone specialist.
Brother: Why?
Sister: Because you've certainly got the head
for it.

☆ ☆ ☆

When the father called home, his six-year-old
son answered and said, "Don't talk too
loud, Dad, the babysitter is asleep."

☆ ☆ ☆

Your conscience is the thing that makes you
tell your mother before your sister does.

☆ ☆ ☆

Brother: I hear that fish is brain food.
Sister: You had better eat a whale.

☆ ☆ ☆

The longest word in the English language is
the one that follows, "And now a word
from our sponsor."

☆ ☆ ☆

Hotel Guest: Can you give me a room and a
bath, please?
Porter: I can give you a room, but you'll have
to wash yourself.

☆ ☆ ☆

Two friends who lived in the town were chat-
ting. "I've just bought a pig," said the first.
"But where will you keep it?" said the
second. "Your yard's much too small for a
pig!"
"I'm going to keep it under my bed," replied
his friend.
"But what about the smell?"
"He'll soon get used to that."

☆ ☆ ☆

Tom: Yesterday I bought three plants. I
planted one in my yard, another in my

neighbor's yard, and the third in my other neighbor's yard.

Jerry: Why did you do that?

Tom: The nursery said to plant them a yard apart.

☆ ☆ ☆

Blow: Yesterday I dropped an egg five stories without breaking it.

Joe: How could you do that?

Blow: I dropped it six stories.

☆ ☆ ☆

Owner: My dog is a nuisance. He chases everyone on a bicycle. What can I do?

Vet: Take his bike away.

☆ ☆ ☆

Sylvester: If you were making an omelet, would you choose chicken eggs or elephant eggs?

Tweety: Chicken eggs because elephant yolks are usually terrible!

☆ ☆ ☆

A woman entered a beauty parlor with a
rabbit on her head.

"How can I help you?" asked the beautician,
trying not to notice the animal on top of
the woman's head.

"Well," said the woman, "you can start by
teasing my hare."

☆ ☆ ☆

Grandfather: Uh, oh! I just made an illegal
right turn.

Grandson: That's okay, Grandpa. The police
car behind you did the same thing.

☆ ☆ ☆

Tourist: This is a steep drop-off. Why don't
you put up a fence and danger sign?

Resident: We did have a sign once, but
nobody fell off, so we took it down.

☆ ☆ ☆

Mother: Let me see your report card, Robert.

Robert: Here it is, Mother, but don't show it
to Dad. He's been helping me.

☆ ☆ ☆

Man: Some girls think I'm handsome and some girls think I'm ugly. What do you think?

Woman: A bit of both. Pretty ugly.

☆ ☆ ☆

Clerk: Would you like to buy a pocket calculator?

Customer: No, thanks. I know how many pockets I have.

☆ ☆ ☆

First boy: I can't understand why people say my girlfriend's legs look like matchsticks.

Second boy: They do look like sticks, but they certainly don't match.

40

Mavis and Mable

Mavis: What's the difference between a camel
and a strawberry?
Mable: I don't know.
Mavis: A strawberry is red.

☆ ☆ ☆

Mavis: What did the rooster whisper?
Mable: I have no idea.
Mavis: Mycrowsoft.

☆ ☆ ☆

Mavis: What kind of computers do Chi-
huahuas like best?

Mable: You tell me.
Mavis: Laptop!

☆ ☆ ☆

Mavis: What kind of orange can float?
Mable: I give up.
Mavis: A naval orange.

☆ ☆ ☆

Mavis: What do you do if you split your sides
laughing?
Mable: Who knows?
Mavis: Run until you get a stitch.

☆ ☆ ☆

Mavis: What happens if you tell a psychiatrist
you are schizophrenic?
Mable: You've got me.
Mavis: He charges you double.

☆ ☆ ☆

Mavis: What happens when a frog's car
breaks down?
Mable: I give up.
Mavis: It gets toad away.

☆ ☆ ☆

Mavis: What does a comedian eat for breakfast?
Mable: Who knows?
Mavis: Puncakes.

☆ ☆ ☆

Mavis: What do you get when you cross a dog and a computer?
Mable: You've got me.
Mavis: A machine that has a bark worse than its byte.

☆ ☆ ☆

Mavis: What did the doctor say to you yesterday?
Mable: He said I was allergic to horses.
Mavis: I've never heard of anyone suffering from that. What's the condition called?
Mable: Bronco-itis.

☆ ☆ ☆

Mavis: What is the prettiest vegetable?
Mable: My mind is blank.
Mavis: Cutecumber.

☆ ☆ ☆

Mavis: What is another name for a juvenile
    delinquent?
Mable: That's a mystery.
Mavis: Child hood.

☆ ☆ ☆

Mavis: What would you get if you crossed a
    comedian with a termite?
Mable: I don't have the foggiest.
Mavis: A joker who brings down the house.

☆ ☆ ☆

Mavis: What do you call a talkative monkey?
Mable: It's unknown to me.
Mavis: A blaboon.

☆ ☆ ☆

Mavis: What part of your body has the best
    sense of humor?
Mable: I'm blank.
Mavis: Your funny bone.

☆ ☆ ☆

Mavis: What did the bus conductor say to the frog?
Mable: Search me.
Mavis: Hop on.

41

Knee-slappers

Veterinarian: Nurse, why are there 101 dalmatians in the office?

Nurse: They all have the same problem. They keep seeing spots before their eyes.

☆ ☆ ☆

Mother to fussy son: Twenty years from now you'll be telling some girl what a great cook your mother was. Now eat your dinner.

☆ ☆ ☆

Dolly: My father plays the piano by ear. How about yours?

Molly: Mine fiddles with his mustache.

☆ ☆ ☆

Henry: Please, Dr. Mindwarp! I can't go
back to my new classroom. I think I'm a
needle!
Doctor: Hmmmm. I see your point!

☆ ☆ ☆

Handsome Harry: Every time I walk past a
girl she sighs.
Wisecracking William: With relief!

☆ ☆ ☆

Vegetarian: I've lived on nothing but vegeta-
bles for years.
Bored listener: That's nothing. I've lived on
Earth all my life.

☆ ☆ ☆

Hiker: Are we lost?
Guide: Of course not. We're here. It's the trail
that's lost.

☆ ☆ ☆

A man answered his doorbell and a friend
walked in, followed by a very large dog.

As they began talking, the dog knocked over a lamp, jumped up on the sofa with his muddy feet, and began chewing on one of the pillows.

The outraged householder, unable to contain himself any longer, burst out, "Don't you think you should train your dog better?"

"My dog!" exclaimed the friend, surprised. "I thought it was your dog."

☆ ☆ ☆

Sign in school cafeteria: Shoes Are Required to Eat in the Cafeteria.

Someone wrote below: Socks Can Eat Wherever They Want.

☆ ☆ ☆

Donna: Please, Dr. Mindwarp! I can't go back to my new classroom. I think I'm a pair of curtains!

Doctor: Please, Donna! Pull yourself together.

☆ ☆ ☆

An idiot decided to start a chicken farm, so he bought a hundred chickens to begin with.

A month later he returned to the dealer for another hundred chickens because all of the first lot had died. A month later he was back at the dealer for another hundred chickens, for the second lot had also died. "But I think I know where I'm going wrong," said the idiot, "I think I'm planting them too deep."

☆ ☆ ☆

Cabdriver: Lady, that 25-cent tip you gave me was an insult.
Lady: How much should I tip you?
Cabdriver: Another 25 cents.
Lady: I wouldn't think of insulting you twice.

☆ ☆ ☆

Two wrongs don't make a right. But what did two Wrights make?
The first airplane.

☆ ☆ ☆

Sister: The police are looking for a thief with one eye.
Brother: Why don't they use two eyes?

☆ ☆ ☆

Brian: Our school must have very clean
    kitchens.
Bill: How can you tell?
Brian: All the food tastes like soap.

☆ ☆ ☆

Two neighbors were having a chat across the
    garden fence. "My son's learning to play
    football," said one.
"Oh, really," said the other. "What position
    does he play?"
"The coach says he's a drawback."

☆ ☆ ☆

First Spider: I'm sorry I'm late for lunch, but
    I was answering my e-mail.
Second Spider: You get e-mail? How come?
First Spider: I'm on the web.

42

Waiter, Waiter

Customer: Waiter, did you know this coffee is very weak?
Waiter: It's been sick.

☆ ☆ ☆

Customer: Waiter, can you do something about this fly in my soup?
Waiter: I'll call the bouncer.

☆ ☆ ☆

Customer: Waiter, waiter! There's a cockroach on my steak.
Waiter: They don't seem to care what they eat, do they, sir?

☆ ☆ ☆

Customer: Waiter, waiter, what's this cockroach doing on my ice-cream sundae?
Waiter: I think it's skiing downhill.

☆ ☆ ☆

Customer: Waiter, waiter, there's a dead
beetle in my gravy.
Waiter: Yes, sir. Beetles are terrible swimmers.

☆ ☆ ☆

Customer: Waiter, waiter! There's a fly in my
bean soup.
Waiter: Don't worry, sir, I'll take it back and
exchange it for a bean.

☆ ☆ ☆

Customer: Waiter, couldn't you make this
corned beef lean?
Waiter: Which way?

☆ ☆ ☆

Customer: Waiter, is there soup on the menu?
Waiter: No, ma'am, I wiped it off.

☆ ☆ ☆

Customer: Waiter, waiter! Have you got
frogs' legs?
Waiter: No, sir, I always walk like this.

☆ ☆ ☆

Customer: Waiter, waiter! Did you know
there is a fly in my soup?
Waiter: That's not a fly, sir. It's just dirt in the
shape of a fly.

☆ ☆ ☆

Customer: Waiter, waiter! There's a fly in my
soup!
Waiter: Just wait until you see the main
course.

☆ ☆ ☆

Customer: Waiter, waiter! What is this fly
doing in the alphabet soup?
Waiter: Learning to spell.

☆ ☆ ☆

Customer: Waiter, this food isn't fit for a pig!
Waiter: All right, I'll get you some that is.

☆ ☆ ☆

Customer: Waiter, waiter! There are two flies
in my soup.
Waiter: That's all right, sir. Have the extra
one on me.

☆ ☆ ☆

Customer: Waiter, I must say that I don't like
all the flies in this dining room!
Waiter: Tell me which ones you don't like,
and I'll chase them out for you.

☆ ☆ ☆

Customer: There's a dead fly in my soup.
Waiter: I know. It's the heat that kills them.

43

Daphne and Darby

Daphne: What do you call singing insects?
Darby: I have no clue.
Daphne: Humbugs.

☆ ☆ ☆

Daphne: What do you call Judge Snake?
Darby: I don't know.
Daphne: Hiss honor.

☆ ☆ ☆

Daphne: What's the best day to talk?
Darby: I can't guess.
Daphne: Chatterday.

☆ ☆ ☆

Daphne: What did one shoe say to the other?
Darby: I have no idea.
Daphne: Your lace is familiar.

☆ ☆ ☆

Daphne: What do you call two graphs?
Darby: You tell me.
Daphne: A paragraph.

☆ ☆ ☆

Daphne: What is black, white, brown, and red
all over?
Darby: I give up.
Daphne: A Chihuahua in a tuxedo that tripped
into a jar of salsa.

☆ ☆ ☆

Daphne: What happened to the frog who was
parked illegally in front of the school?
Darby: Who knows?
Daphne: It got toad away.

☆ ☆ ☆

Daphne: What powerful reptile has a dog
  named Toto?
Darby: You've got me.
Daphne: The Lizard of Oz.

☆ ☆ ☆

Daphne: What is the best way to keep fish
  from smelling?
Darby: My mind is blank.
Daphne: Cut off their noses.

☆ ☆ ☆

Daphne: What happened after Old King Cole
  ordered his men to mix chopped cabbage
  with mayonnaise?
Darby: That's a mystery.
Daphne: It became known as Cole's Law.

☆ ☆ ☆

Daphne: What is the favorite drink of cats?
Darby: I don't have the foggiest.
Daphne: Mice tea.

☆ ☆ ☆

Daphne: What Native American tribe has the
  most lawyers?

Darby: It's unknown to me.
Daphne: The Sioux.

☆ ☆ ☆

Daphne: What did the bee say to the flower?
Darby: I'm blank.
Daphne: Hello, honey.

☆ ☆ ☆

Daphne: What could happen if I get a frog in
my throat?
Darby: You might croak.

☆ ☆ ☆

Daphne: What do you get when you cross an
elephant with a computer?
Darby: I'm in the dark.
Daphne: A 5000-pound know-it-all!

☆ ☆ ☆

Daphne: What did you do after Joe gave you
the hot foot?
Darby: I gave him the cold shoulder.

☆ ☆ ☆

Daphne: What's the difference between your new teacher and a train?

Darby: How should I know?

Daphne: Your new teacher says, "Spit out your gum!" But a train says, "Choo! Choo!"

☆ ☆ ☆

Daphne: What did the shoe salesman do when he got a computer?

Darby: Beats me.

Daphne: He booted up.

☆ ☆ ☆

Daphne: What road do tiny biting insects travel on?

Darby: I have no clue.

Daphne: The flea way.

44

How Come?

Employer: How's your spelling? Let me hear you spell *Mississippi*.
Secretary: The river or the state?

☆ ☆ ☆

Noel: How do roofers march in a parade?
Evan: I have no clue.
Noel: In shingle file.

☆ ☆ ☆

Sam: How can you tell your computer is getting old?
Ram: I don't know.
Sam: It loses its memory.

☆ ☆ ☆

Boy: How does Jack Frost get to work?
Girl: I can't guess.
Boy: By icicle.

☆ ☆ ☆

Customer: How much for a slice of cake?
Waitress: Sixty-six cents.
Customer: How much for a slice of upside-
down cake?
Waitress: Ninety-nine cents.

☆ ☆ ☆

Melinda: What do you use for smelly rabbits?
Julie: I have no idea.
Melinda: Hare freshener.

☆ ☆ ☆

Brent: How do you repair an orchestra?
Russ: You tell me.
Brent: With Band-Aids.

☆ ☆ ☆

Jack: How come you go fishing every day?
John: I can't help it. I'm hooked.

☆ ☆ ☆

Emily: How do you know which zebra can
 ride a bike?
Timeka: I give up.
Emily: It's the one wearing a helmet!

☆ ☆ ☆

Steve: How did the kangaroo get into the
 school?
Kevin: Who knows?
Steve: It opened the door.

☆ ☆ ☆

Kim: How would you like to take your cod-
 liver oil?
Hannah: With a fork!

☆ ☆ ☆

Seth: How do you make a milk shake?
Abby: You've got me.
Seth: Give it a good scare.

☆ ☆ ☆

Kim: How do you make a Yankee doodle?
Mark: It's unknown to me.
Kim: Give him a pencil.

☆ ☆ ☆

Claire: How can you make a turtle fast?
Chad: I don't have the foggiest.
Claire: Take away its food!

45

I've Got a Question

Mother: Why is there a strange baby in the
crib?
Daughter: You told me to change the baby.

☆ ☆ ☆

Mother: Why did Mickey Mouse take a trip to
outer space?
Daughter: I'm blank.
Mother: He wanted to find Pluto.

☆ ☆ ☆

Nate: Why did the boy ride his camel to
school?

Julia: Because his horse was too heavy to
carry!

☆ ☆ ☆

Husband: Why did you take the clock to the
psychiatrist?
Wife: It was a cuckoo clock.

☆ ☆ ☆

Brother: Why didn't the skeleton go to the
party?
Sister: Search me.
Brother: He had no body to go with.

☆ ☆ ☆

Danny: Why are you jumping up and down?
Kari: I don't know.
Danny: Did you just drink some spring water?

☆ ☆ ☆

Christian: Why is an island like the letter *T?*
Christy: You've got me guessing.
Christian: Because they're both in the middle
of water.

☆ ☆ ☆

Art: Why are black panthers black?
Judy: How should I know?
Art: So you can tell them apart from
    flamingos.

☆ ☆ ☆

Erin: Why did the computer sneeze?
Anna: Beats me.
Erin: It had a virus.

☆ ☆ ☆

Edward: Why did the burglar take a shower?
Rusty: I have no clue.
Edward: He wanted to make a clean getaway.

☆ ☆ ☆

Bill: Why didn't the piecrust get a job?
Caron: I don't know.
Bill: It was too flaky.

☆ ☆ ☆

Coach: Why did you miss that shot?
Player: I sprained my ankle.
Coach: That's a lame excuse.

☆ ☆ ☆

Teacher: Why shouldn't you take a cow to a zoo?

Student: I can't guess.

Teacher: Because she would rather go to the movies.

46

Why, Why, Why?

Judge: Why did you steal three TVs?
Accused: I specialize in multimedia.

☆ ☆ ☆

Boyfriend: Why didn't you give me anything
for my birthday?
Girlfriend: You told me to surprise you.

☆ ☆ ☆

Patient: Why did you charge me a group rate?
Psychiatrist: You've got multiple personali-
ties.

☆ ☆ ☆

Judge: Why did you rob the same store twice?
Robber: I had double coupons.

☆ ☆ ☆

Student: Why did the spider go to computer class?
Computer Teacher: It was searching for a new web site.

☆ ☆ ☆

Terry: Why did the rabbit get so mad?
Sherry: I give up.
Terry: She was having a bad hare day.

☆ ☆ ☆

Larry: Why do women paint their nails?
Barry: Who knows?
Larry: It's easier than wallpapering them.

☆ ☆ ☆

Wendy: Why did the bear go over the mountain?
Steve: You've got me.
Wendy: He couldn't go under it.

☆ ☆ ☆

Makena: Why did the crow sit on the telephone line?

Kyler: My mind is a blank.

Makena: Because he was making a long-distance caw.

☆ ☆ ☆

Mindy: Why did the silly kid buy a thousand pickles?

Cindy: That's a mystery.

Mindy: He got a good dill.

☆ ☆ ☆

Adam: Why did the horse go to the doctor?

Noah: I don't have the foggiest.

Adam: For hay fever.

47

School Humor

Teacher: Give, for one year, the number of tons of coal shipped out of the United States.
Student: 1498: none.

☆ ☆ ☆

Teacher: You missed school yesterday, didn't you?
Student: Not a bit.

☆ ☆ ☆

Teacher: Can you give me a good example of how heat expands things and cold contracts them?

Student: Well, the days are much longer in
the summer.

☆ ☆ ☆

Teacher: What is the axis of the earth?
Student: The axis of the earth is an imaginary
line which passes from one pole to the
other, and on which the earth revolves.
Teacher: Very good. Now, could you hang
clothes on that line?
Student: Yes, sir.
Teacher: Indeed, and what sort of clothes?
Student: Imaginary clothes, sir.

☆ ☆ ☆

Teacher: In which of his battles was King
Alexander XIV of Smogaria slain?
Student: I'm pretty sure it was the last one.

☆ ☆ ☆

Teacher: What's the formula for water?
Student: H, I, J, K, L, M, N, O.
Teacher: That's not the formula I gave you.
Student: Yes, it is. You said it was H to O.

☆ ☆ ☆

Teacher: What do you call a person who keeps on talking when people are no longer interested?

Student: A teacher.

✩ ✩ ✩

Computer Teacher: Eugene, why does your Apple computer have teeth marks on it?

Eugene: I think someone took a few bytes out of it.

✩ ✩ ✩

Teacher: Are you good at arithmetic?

Student: Well, yes and no.

Teacher: What do you mean, yes and no?

Student: Yes, I'm no good at arithmetic.

✩ ✩ ✩

Teacher: One of your essays is very good, but the other one I can't read.

Student: Yes, sir. My mother is a much better writer than my father.

✩ ✩ ✩

Science Teacher: The law of gravity keeps us from falling off the earth.

Student: What kept us from falling off before the law was passed?

☆ ☆ ☆

Teacher: Please give me the definition of climate.

Student: What kids do when they see a tree!

48

Who's There?

Knock, knock.
Who's there?
Howard.
Howard who?
Howard you like me to keep knocking on
 your door?

☆ ☆ ☆

Knock, knock.
Who's there?
Wheelbarrow.
Wheelbarrow who?
Wheelbarrow some money and buy a new car.

☆ ☆ ☆

Knock, knock.
Who's there?
Tuna.
Tuna who?
Tuna sandwich with potato chips, please.

☆ ☆ ☆

Knock, knock.
Who's there?
Cindy.
Cindy who?
Cindy someone to open the door.

☆ ☆ ☆

Knock, knock.
Who's there?
Lettuce.
Lettuce who?
Lettuce in and we'll tell you.

☆ ☆ ☆

Knock, knock.
Who's there?
Micky.
Micky who?
Micky is lost so that's why I'm knocking.

☆ ☆ ☆

Knock, knock.
Who's there?
Goliath.
Goliath who?
Goliath down and take a nap.

☆ ☆ ☆

Knock, knock.
Who's there?
Ya.
Ya who?
Ya who. I'm having fun, are you?

☆ ☆ ☆

Knock, knock.
Who's there?
Sacha.
Sacha who?
Sacha fuss, just because I knocked at your door.

☆ ☆ ☆

Knock, knock.
Who's there?
Says.

Says who?
Says me, that's who!

☆ ☆ ☆

Knock, knock.
Who's there?
Isabelle.
Isabelle who?
Isabelle broken on the door?

☆ ☆ ☆

Knock, knock.
Who's there?
Stu.
Stu who?
Stu late, I'm not going to tell you.

☆ ☆ ☆

Knock, knock.
Who's there?
Augusta.
Augusta who?
Augusta wind blew my hat off.

☆ ☆ ☆

Knock, knock.
Who's there?
Yule.
Yule who?
Yule never know until you open the door.

☆ ☆ ☆

Knock, knock.
Who's there?
Pollywogs.
Pollywogs who?
Pollywogs her tail. Isn't Polly a good dog?

☆ ☆ ☆

49

Leftovers

Don: I can pick up a cent with only two fingers.
Mike: That's nothing. My dog can do it with
its nose.

☆ ☆ ☆

To discover whether an ostrich is male or
female tell it a joke. If he laughs, it's a
male. If she laughs, it's a female.

☆ ☆ ☆

Guide: If you're lost, tell us your name so that
we can notify your family.
Child: My family knows my name.

☆ ☆ ☆

A blind man went into a shop, picked up his
dog by the tail and swung it around his
head. "Can I help you?" asked the assistant.
"No thanks," said the blind man, "I'm just
looking around."

☆ ☆ ☆

Mom: Go outside and play quietly. Your
father can't read his paper.
Child: Wow, I'm only eight, and I can read it!

☆ ☆ ☆

Patsy: My dog is going to obedience school.
Julie: That's expensive. How can you afford
it?
Patsy: He won a collarship.

☆ ☆ ☆

Mom: Be careful and don't drop that cookie.
Daughter: Why?
Mom: Because chocolate chips.

☆ ☆ ☆

Bill: I've got a splinter in my finger.
Holly: How did you get it . . . scratch your
   head?

☆ ☆ ☆

Amanda: Have you heard the joke about the
   wall?
Haley: You would never get over it.

☆ ☆ ☆

Meagan: The trouble with our teachers is that
   they all do bird impressions.
Cole: Really? What do they do?
Meagan: They watch us like hawks.

☆ ☆ ☆

Wife: Sometimes I think you don't hear a
   word I say.
Husband: What?

☆ ☆ ☆

Woman: Is your taxicab engaged?
Cab Driver: No, but it's going steady.

☆ ☆ ☆

Customer: You call this beef noodle soup
your special? I can't find any beef or
noodles in it.
Waiter: That's why it's special.

☆ ☆ ☆

Sergeant: Soldier, your bunk is a disgrace.
Soldier: I know, but it's the only one you
gave me.

☆ ☆ ☆

Mother: I see you got another bad report card.
Child: A teacher's job is to teach. Why should
I get the blame if she fails?

☆ ☆ ☆

Nit: Can you ice-skate?
Wit: I don't know—I can't stand up long
enough to find out.

☆ ☆ ☆

Jacob: I have an uncle who lives in Alaska.
Maria: Nome?
Jacob: Sure, I know him. He's my uncle!

Other Books by Bob Phillips